THERE OR THEREABOUTS
The Keith Alexander Story

Rob Bradley

Vertical Editions
www.verticaleditions.com

First published in the United Kingdom in 2012 by Vertical Editions, Unit 4a, Snaygill Industrial Estate, Skipton, North Yorkshire BD23 2QR

www.verticaleditions.com

ISBN 978-1-904091-66-0

A CIP catalogue record for this book is available from the British Library

Cover design by HBA, York

Printed and bound by MPG, Bodmin

To Matt, Paul, Jack and Jenny
And to the memory of Richard Butcher

Contents

Acknowledgements

I'd like to acknowledge the following organisations for their help with archive information and photographs: Grahame Lloyd/Celluloid Publishing (*One Hell of a Season*), *Grimsby Telegraph*, Lincoln City FC, *Lincolnshire Echo*, Macclesfield Town FC and Peterborough United FC

I'd also like to thank all the people who helped with *There or Thereabouts* and spoke so willingly and helpfully about Keith, including: Gary Birtles, John Blackwell, Aidy Boothroyd, Jim Boyce, Grant Brown, John Cockerill, Leigh Curtis, Tony Cuthbert, Andy Farrant, Barry Fry, Malcolm Hird, Michael Hortin, Andy King, Alan Marriott, Karl Mercer, Paul Morgan, Alan Parker, Gary Parle, Geoffrey Piper, Mike Rance, Keith Rudd, Ben Sedgemore, Gary Simpson, Gary Taylor-Fletcher, Steve Thompson, Chris Vaughan, John Vickers and Simon Yeo.

Last, but certainly not least, I'd like to say a special thank you to Helen Alexander and Matt Alexander who shared their memories of Keith with me and made the book possible, and to Grahame Lloyd, Fran Martin and Dawn Robinson for all their kind help in putting Keith's story together.

Rob Bradley
July 2012

Foreword

Although the name of Keith Alexander may not immediately be recognised by all football supporters, his untimely loss back in March 2010 was sadly received by a large section from within the 'football family' of clubs, managers, coaches, players and fans. When I attended his funeral it was clear his contribution as a player and coach had touched many a person, which I am sure would have pleasantly surprised even Keith himself, who probably never realised how his reputation had grown to the level it had.

My own link had only occurred during his latter years when I joined The Football Association and he was involved in our coaching programmes. He was definitely a key 'standard-bearer' for those who wanted to see recognition for an increase in black coaches within the ninety two professional clubs of the Premier League and the Football League.

More importantly he understood the necessity of working hard to gain his qualifications and experience as a coach rather than just sit back and complain of no opportunities coming his way. In fact the whole basis of his successful life was that commitment to lead by example, setting himself standards and aspirations which undoubtedly inspired those around him. The ultimate accolade was of course his popularity with football fans, who are never easily fooled, and love nothing better than seeing someone who wears their heart on their sleeve.

Everything Keith achieved during his career was very much down to sheer hard work and there is nothing better that seeing such inner belief being rewarded. His individual pathway should act as an inspiration for everyone, because he overcame numerous challenges, frustrations and disappointments which could have defeated many, but each time he bounced back with even greater determination.

He played for numerous non-league clubs before becoming a full-time professional player, and then again his managerial career was another fascinating rollercoaster ride. We so often read about the high profile personalities within football and the financial excesses which create the wrong sort of media headlines. This particular book highlights the other side of our national game, where a charismatic leader can impact on so many individuals and community groups by their willingness to encourage and squeeze the maximum out of those around them.

Keith came through a generation within football where racism was a factor as a player and a manager, but who helped improve our understanding of how education and tolerance was the way forward. Soon after his sad loss, the football season 2011-12 saw a couple of unfortunate reminders that must never allow us to be complacent about progress made in this area. I am sure his wise counsel and thought would have been sought because he was a rare, genuine and decent man who gained huge respect for the person he was, rather than where he was from.

Sir Trevor Brooking CBE
July 2012

1

Shoestring Squad but Success with the Imps

". . . and our first job will be to stay in the Football League,
particularly now it's two teams to go down . . ."
Keith Alexander

In May 2002, thirty or so football fans travelled to the High Court in Birmingham to sit nervously in the public gallery and witness if Lincoln City's petition to enter administration would be granted, ensuring that their beloved club had a chance of survival. In May 2003, thousands upon thousands of Imps fans made their way to the Millennium Stadium in Cardiff to watch their team attempt to win the League Two play-off final. From the club's financial meltdown and the brink of extinction, manager Keith Alexander proudly led his young squad out on to the pitch to the sound of fireworks and razzmatazz for a play-off showdown and the brink of promotion.

"These lads should be named team of the season for what they've done," said Keith before the game. "We were favourites to go down at the start of the season. Other clubs that have gone into administration haven't had the problems we've had. Eight of this squad are out of non-league and they've all been magnificent. We're a decent team with some good players, despite what some people might have said. Hopefully we've made our fans happy by getting here and we need to go on and win it."

As the teams lined up before kick-off, and remembering the

trials and tribulations of the previous twelve months, there was hardly a dry eye in the house among the hordes of Lincoln City fans standing there paying tribute to their manager, the man responsible for this remarkable transformation, and his team.

*****

Keith had rejoined Lincoln City at the start of the 2001-02 season as assistant to manager Alan Buckley, having previously had a brief period there as manager in the mid-90s. The previous owner, John Reames, had stood down after many years at the helm. The club had become owned by the 'community' in the form of the supporters trust and local business people, including Lincolnshire Co-operative. I had been on the board as a fans' representative for a short time, and was made acting chairman as the transition from a single owner to the new much broader ownership model took place. Once the new board was in place, I stayed on as chairman proper.

Impressed by Buckley's success as a manager at lower league level and his insistence on playing attractive passing football, our new board was quick to recruit him, having already relieved current manager Phil Stant of his duties. Buckley's request to bring in Keith was readily granted as he was well thought of from his previous spells there as both a player and manager. Sadly, over the next year or so, the full extent of debt at the club became known, which the infamous ITV Digital collapse made worse, and the threat of insolvency became more and more real. By then the board was taking advice from insolvency practitioners and, after the last game of the 2001-02 season at Hull, Alan Buckley became one of a number of victims of the spending cuts the board had to make. Whilst Buckley's appointment was made for all the right football reasons, the board was now concentrating solely on financial matters and, when Keith confirmed he'd take over the managerial reins and be prepared to do so on the same salary he was paid as an assistant, we were quick to award him the post. Keith, however, was wary.

"Under John Reames in my first spell, I learned quickly never to trust what a chairman has to say," he revealed. "At our weekly meetings, he'd insist that it didn't matter where we finished as long as the younger players had a good season and developed into first team regulars. We would really go for it next season, I was told. We were losing lots of games 1-0 but results didn't bother me because we were playing some lovely football. Then I was sacked. I also learned that playing too much good football can damage your health in the bottom division. I felt I was unfairly dismissed, but that's football. I didn't think a year was long enough and we were developing a good team with some good youngsters who would go on to make the club a lot of money, which is exactly what I'd been asked to do."

To be fair to Keith, and to some members of the board, he wasn't made manager second time round entirely to save money. During conversations on the team bus, for example, after Alan Buckley had been dropped off near to his home in North Lincolnshire, Keith often hinted that success at lower league level could be achieved in ways that didn't always involve established league players and slick passing tactics. Whilst he'd remained firmly loyal to his boss's football principles and methods at the time, these views suddenly seemed attractive to the directors.

The thought of good, young and inexpensive players with an up-and-at-'em style of play as described by Keith might just be the way to survive on the pitch when the fight for survival off it was going on at the same time. So Keith Alexander was appointed manager of Lincoln City for a second time. He revealed later that he felt he might have earned that chance at some stage in the future, although not under the same circumstances.

"I thought I'd become manager here one day because I felt

we'd do well and Alan would move on," he said. "I couldn't see myself leaving unless Alan moved to a bigger club and wanted to take me with him. When he was sacked, I was offered another opportunity to manage in the League, albeit a difficult one. I know what they say about never going back and I knew that if I failed at this job, I wouldn't get another chance in the Football League."

One of the reasons Keith was pleased he was staying with the club was that he lived locally and he would be unhappy at uprooting his young children, Jack and Jenny. Matt Alexander, his grown-up son from his first marriage, confirmed this.

"Dad didn't want Helen and the kids to have to move house and change schools," he said. "He'd had enough travelling around. But the other big reason he was keen to take on the manager's job was that he wanted to show what he could do. He'd got a chance in the League and he wanted to prove he could do it, and do it well."

"Keith was uneasy taking on an assistant's job," confirmed Helen. "It was a big decision after already having the manager's job at Northwich. He was also coaching for Alan knowing that trying to play pretty football wasn't working. So he was delighted to be offered the top job. He wanted to prove, after the last time, he could get results. It was lovely for us as a family. The club was down the road, Keith would do the school run, and he was happy. He was relishing the challenge."

Vice-chairman Jim Hicks was happy too. He was the only member of the current board who'd been a director when Keith was appointed manager for the first time. Keith and he had become good friends then, and the decision to sack him was made when Jim and his wife, Shirley, were in Spain. He was therefore unable to be involved in the discussions that led to that drastic action. He was pleased Keith had been given another chance even though the circumstances this time were very tough.

Keith's first job was to appoint an assistant. It was the first of many challenges because his playing budget was now only a fraction of the sum allocated to his former boss. There was only one candidate, though, and Gary Simpson joined the club having performed the same role with Keith at Ilkeston and Northwich. When Keith had accepted Buckley's offer to join him at Sincil Bank, it split up his working partnership with Gary, but they kept in touch. Gary spent a lot of time watching non-league games and had built up a dossier of young talented players.

Years before, he had played for Boston United, briefly with Keith at one stage, and appeared for them at Wembley in the FA Trophy final in 1985. He had also managed Gainsborough Trinity in the '90s, so he already had a good knowledge of the non-league scene. Gary was to carry out his job on a part-time basis and was to receive a modest wage of a couple of hundred pounds a week which he would augment by continuing to run his business selling sun-beds. Keith Oakes, a former player with Peterborough, Newport, Gillingham and Fulham and the current physiotherapist, was kept on, and it was decided he would help Keith and Gary with coaching, over and above his medical duties.

"Keith is a good physio who knows football inside out," said Keith the manager. "I know I'm going to be on my own a lot of the time so I asked him to be more involved. He'll look after the defenders one day a week and if I see things in a match I'm not happy with, then he'll work on them for me."

Oakes said, "I'm asked for my opinion and it's nice to have some input in training. Now everybody is pulling in the same direction and that's something you don't find at every club. We're all in it together and three heads are better than one."

With a much reduced budget, the three heads certainly had some thinking to do. Keith needed new players and the only way he was going to get them was by moving on some of the existing highest paid ones. One or two of the current contracts stood out as more than excessive during the austere period the club found itself in. Players were on four figures a week with bonuses for only doing a reasonable job. One gained a lump sum 'signing-on' fee each summer even though he was already guaranteed a deal the following year. Where possible, the board made the high earners offers so that they could be paid off. Even so, the new wage structure wouldn't allow established Football League players to be recruited, or even those out of the highest non-league circles. So Keith and Gary looked further down the ladder because those lads were affordable, and they already knew of a few who would do a job for them.

Club secretary Fran Martin soon became busy as, one after another, new players arrived. Keith recruited giant centre-half Ben Futcher, son of former Manchester City star Paul, from Stalybridge, along with Simon Weaver, who he had recommended without success to Alan Buckley the season before. Scott Willis, whose previous claim to fame was that he was Cilla Black's nephew, came from Droylsden, Dene Cropper was signed from Worksop and striker Simon Yeo, aged twenty-eight, came from Hyde United. Mark Camm, a squad player who hadn't previously been offered a contract to stay on, was given one by Keith. Perhaps remembering long ago in his early playing days at Stamford when his team-mates all seemed like giants, Keith was keen to bring in big strong young lads.

Whilst the wages at the club were now much reduced, the new players were keen to sign and have a chance at League football under a manager they admired. Two existing players, Paul Smith and Richard Logan, who had both suffered serious back injuries, were kept on by Keith when they might have thought their careers were over.

"Simon is an out-and-out goal-scorer, which is something this club has lacked for a number of years," explained Keith. "At his age, it's a last chance for him to make it in the Football League. Dene is only nineteen and a player for the future. Ben is a very big centre-back who will be a handful for people in our division, and we should have brought Simon Weaver here last year. They're all players who I think will be useful at this level and they all come well within our budget."

As well as bringing in new players, Keith and Gary spent a lot of time persuading highly paid members of the existing squad like Kingsley Black, Tony Battersby and Ian Hamilton, that they might fare better elsewhere, especially if they could reach some sort of financial agreement with the club first. That way they would receive a one-off lump sum, the club would save on PAYE and NI payments and, if they were to get fixed up at another club, they would, of course, be paid there too and may be even better off. More importantly they might well be playing football, which would be unlikely under Keith and Gary. Lee Thorpe, the previous season's leading scorer and someone they would have preferred to keep if his wages had been lower, left for Orient who agreed to take over his existing contract.

Slowly a squad began to take shape. Keith soon decided that, although his players had strength, pace, and spirit, he wouldn't be asking Gary to coach them to play lots of elaborate football in a 4-4-2 formation. It would be a 5-3-2 set-up with three centre-halves and speedy full-backs, not conceding being the first priority, not letting their opponents play, lots of long throws into the opposition penalty area and generally getting the ball forward where possible. Good football would follow once those methods had started to work and confidence grew. The main priority, though, was creating an excellent team spirit. If they could establish an 'all for one, one for all' attitude, Keith and Gary knew it would be worth at least fifteen points in the season that followed. And those points might easily be the difference between staying in the Football League or getting relegated.

As the squad was assembled and started to gel, it also became clear that the partnership of Keith, Gary, and Keith Oakes was starting the process of making an impact in the professional game. Of course, Keith and Gary had worked together before, but their ideas and their methods were already developing into something that would stand out in the lower reaches of the Football League. As the new season approached, a lot of people at other clubs didn't know what the hell was going to hit them when they prepared for their game against little Lincoln City and an expected haul of three easy points.

*****

With the club having come out of administration just five days earlier, directors sitting on the team coach waiting to set off for the first match of the season at Kidderminster had already noticed an improvement. In the corresponding fixture last time round, players had got word of possible financial problems, including a report in a national newspaper saying that they might not get paid. They'd refused to get on the bus and it took a fair bit of diplomacy and persuasion to get them to climb aboard. As they left the ground for the start of the 2002-03 season, the directors didn't know, after concentrating solely on financial matters all summer, whether the team was going to be any good. They feared a close season of struggle behind the scenes was going to be followed by months of struggling on the pitch at the wrong end of the table. Not only that, but a rule change had not been lost on Keith Alexander.

"Nobody is expecting us to tear up any trees and our first job will be to stay in the Football League, particularly now it's two teams to go down," he said. "It's a pity the two down rule has been brought in just as I've taken over as manager!"

This wasn't lost on the board and the fans, too, especially as Lincoln City had a habit of breaking unwanted records, including being the first club to suffer when automatic relegation for one club was introduced in 1986. As it was, they were more than pleasantly surprised as a battling away side more than matched their hosts in the bright sunshine at Aggborough. Richard Logan put the Imps ahead but Kidderminster soon equalised. Then Alan Marriott, tipped by his manager to dive to his left, saved a penalty as the Imps held on for a draw, despite Dene Cropper being sent off late on. Suddenly it started to dawn on people that Lincoln City might have a half decent team, and not only that, one that they could identify with and feel a part of. One where hard work and team spirit bonded everyone together, including the fans.

After a home victory against Rochdale, the next two games were full of incident. Carlisle won at Sincil Bank despite having three players sent off. Their chairman got into the act too, his misbehaviour in the directors seating area leading to him being escorted out of the ground by police officers. This led to ill feeling between both clubs for some time. Then Lincoln lost at Boston in the eagerly awaited first-ever Football League Lincolnshire derby, and again indiscipline rather than football was making the headlines. Keith was keen that his team were aggressive and played a high tempo game, but striker Simon Yeo was the latest to go a bit too far and was shown a red card after kicking out at an opponent.

"That was ludicrous and Simon will pay for it with a fine," raged his manager. "He gets frustrated but he's a professional footballer now and he needs to concentrate on scoring goals. It cost us the game." Calming down, he explained again his aims for the club. "Team Lincoln is something I'm trying to foster. I encouraged a similar thing at Ilkeston and Northwich. I've never been at a club that's fashionable or got a lot of money so you need team spirit. The players need to get on, the backroom staff must be part of the set-up, and you need the office staff to feel wanted too. Whatever needs doing will get done by anyone and everyone."

The team ethic began to work and Lincoln won the next three games. As winter approached they were well placed in the top six. The back five were doing their job and one of them, Ben Futcher, was contributing at the other end by scoring goals from set-pieces. Peter Gain, who had been with the club for a few seasons, had embraced the Alexander way and developed from a tricky winger to a midfielder who created chances when he had the ball and tackled back when he hadn't. Richard Butcher, recruited from Kettering, had the legs to get from box to box and the strength to dominate midfield. Gary Simpson had enjoyed working with Keith before, but he soon recognised how well his manager's methods were working this time.

"The gaffer is laid back," he said "But he knows how to get the best out of everyone. That's a big part of management. He gets the best out of limited resources too. We're contrasting personalities but we complement each other. Almost every game we both pick a different team, for example, and we both argue the merits of the side we've chosen. Then one of us backs down and says we were already thinking of changing it to tally with the other one anyway. We get on, we put the work in, and although we fall out we never bear grudges. We're passionate and we want to succeed."

A Ben Futcher goal in the 75th minute gave Lincoln the lead at Orient, but former Imp Lee Thorpe equalised in the last few seconds to deny them all three points.

"Players always come back to haunt you, don't they?" said Keith, as laid back as ever. "Thorpey was always going to score, but that was fair enough. It was a good goal from a good ball in, and if we'd scored it we would have said it was a great goal. While I'm disappointed to drop the two points, I'm delighted with the team. The lads were excellent from start to finish."

But some people were starting to use words other than 'excellent' though when they spoke about Keith and his team. On a cold Tuesday night, Adie Mike put Lincoln one up at Hartlepool, but the home team replied with two and maintained their position at the top of the league. Chris Turner, their manager, surprised Keith and Gary by being pleasant to their faces at the end of the game, but then derogatory about his opponents' style of play when he spoke to the media. He said that Lincoln had been over-physical and relied on the use of long balls and long throws far too much. At Sincil Bank the next day Keith and Gary made a point of putting a red ring around the return match on the fixture list pinned up on the wall in the manager's office. They decided they'd have plenty to say to their players about Turner's comments when the two teams met next March.

Another member of the Imps squad was having plenty to say too. A couple of years earlier, experienced midfielder Ben Sedgemore was in the Macclesfield team playing Lincoln at Moss Rose when an incident sparked a pitch battle between virtually every member of the two sides. Now he was fully behind his Lincoln team-mates and was full of praise for them after a home draw with near-neighbours Hull City in front of the club's biggest crowd of the season.

"They were flying but we were never outplayed," he said. "We were down to ten men and our backs were against the wall but we dug in. The effort and determination was incredible and I would say it was my most satisfying moment as a player. After the game I heard Peter Taylor, their manager, shouting at his players in the away dressing room. There was plenty of noise coming from our lads too but I heard Peter bellowing that until they had a spirit like we had, they'd never do any good. The atmosphere here is the best I have ever encountered in my career." Ben also had praise for his boss. "Last year we seemed to carry players but that isn't the case this season. The gaffer has done a magnificent job and there are no individuals at all – just teamwork."

The team was undeniably doing well, but the search for new talent was unrelenting. Keith and Gary covered mile after mile night after night attending reserve games and first team matches at all levels, no matter how low in the football pyramid. Keith would turn up, club secretary Fran Martin having arranged a ticket, and he cut a noticeable figure sitting in the stand. He would often have to evade questions about which particular player he was checking out, although often the visit was in the hope of unearthing someone by chance.

Gary, on the other hand, was pleased he was less recognisable, and regularly paid to go through the turnstile and stand and watch with the punters. He felt this gave him a head start if and when it came to contacting a manager to express an interest in a player, especially if that manager wasn't already aware that one of his prospects had already been spotted. The journeys to matches also gave Keith's two grown-up sons a chance to spend some time with their father.

"Dad always met Paul and I to check we were OK. We'd always meet in Starbucks. Dad always had a hot chocolate," said Matt. "And he'd always be on the phone. He was a massive influence and we always asked him for advice. But he never switched off. Not because he was under pressure, but because he loved the game. So I often went to games with him and we could talk in the car."

Matt would soon get to know his father's system for assessing players. "He'd get a team-sheet and if he didn't know the formations straightaway, he'd have them sussed by about a minute into the game. Then he'd mark down all the players who were over six foot tall, along with the ones who were strong, quick, and had quick feet. It was very simple but it worked. He'd also make sure we knew where the hot drinks and sandwiches were at half-time and then, about twenty minutes into the second half, he would say it was time we were off. And we drove home, talking all the way."

As one or two players arrived on the scene, a couple would leave, moved on or out on loan. Keith would often say "You can never have enough strikers" and he'd play them and rest them, rotating the attacking part of the squad to get the best out of them. Scott Willis, apart from driving his manager up the wall by spending his wages in about two days and asking for a sub, or announcing he'd forgotten his boots as the team coach set off for an away trip, was impressing some illustrious people, and it was rumoured Everton were keen. Recognising this and the efforts of all his squad, Keith was quick to push the board to renew some of the players' contracts, especially the ones who were only on a few hundred pounds a week.

The players were aware that attendances at home games were increasing and, although the directors had their hands tied by conditions they had to fulfil as part of coming out of administration, they did all they could. Willis was quick to express his appreciation of his boss for giving him a chance at League football and his enjoyment of the season so far.

"My contract's up soon and the gaffer has mentioned it," he said. "I love it here and I've a great rapport with the fans. I'd sign for ten years if they let me. Keith has been good to me and I respect him a lot. All the lads are a cracking bunch and the dressing room is brilliant."

Whilst things were busy behind the scenes, the action on the pitch was no less eventful. At the Kassam Stadium against Oxford, the Imps hit a brick wall. Despite playing well, they had seven players booked, conceded a disputed last-minute penalty to lose the game, and Keith was sent from the dugout to the stand. The club would be hit by a hefty fine for the bookings and the manager was furious.

"I was ordered to the stand after telling the ref he was useless," said Keith. "He was diabolical and every time we made a tackle we got a booking. He'll go home and not worry about it. He's retiring at the end of the season and it can't come a moment too soon. I gave him seventeen out of fifty in my report."

Despite that setback the team went on a good run, losing only one in eight, including a win at Rochdale that prompted Keith to say: "We were magnificent from start to finish." They then made the long trip to Carlisle in freezing weather in February. It was the second time they'd made that journey, having lost there already in the FA Cup. Revenge was sweet, especially after the events of the home fixture, as the Imps ran out 4-1 winners, including a goal from sixty yards by full-back Mark Bailey, who punted the ball into the home goal after the Carlisle keeper had pushed up for a corner in the last minute. Unknown to Keith, members of the board watched the game exhilarated by the performance, but aware that, on their behalf, I had to give him some bad news the next morning.

Following the ITV Digital debacle, another triumphant Football League deal was failing to come up with the goods, and the FLPTV internet deal was going to bring in £80,000 less than expected. As he entered the boardroom the next morning munching an apple, Keith may have wondered what our meeting was about, but he certainly didn't expect bad news. I explained that, despite the success of the team, the club were having to comply with a financial plan that was agreed in the courts. News that some projected income would be less than promised meant that Keith's budget for next season would have to be reduced.

He was far from happy. He quite rightly said that his players were working miracles and this was unfair on them. Muttering something like "bloody kick in the teeth after winning 4-1", he left the room, leaving a symbolic half-eaten apple on the boardroom table. I reported this back to my fellow directors and, seeing that this had hardly been the most morale-boosting exercise, the board re-assessed and then re-adjusted their forecasts. Keith was then informed that the reduction might not be so drastic after all. This was thankfully received a bit better than the earlier news.

If Keith had been disheartened by this episode, he made sure it didn't rub off on his team. Three days later, players who were more used to grounds at Hyde, Halifax, and Hednesford ran out at Hull's brand spanking new KC Stadium and a Stuart Bimson penalty proved to be the winner. They'd created their own little bit of history by being the first away team to win at a superb ground that, in a few seasons, would be hosting Man Utd, Arsenal, and Chelsea.

Three matches and three draws later, Lincoln hosted high-flying Hartlepool at Sincil Bank. Chris Turner's comments earlier in the season were the only words Keith needed to motivate his players in the dressing room as he sent them out on to the pitch. Hartlepool never got a look-in and looked a dejected bunch as they left the pitch 3-0 losers at the final whistle. Chris Turner had moved on to Sheffield Wednesday a couple of weeks before the match and his replacement Mike Newell's response could not have made a greater contrast to his predecessors end-of-match reaction.

"He shook every one of our players by the hand as they left the pitch," enthused Keith. "I don't know if he knew the history but it was an excellent gesture. He was acknowledging that we played very well on the night."

The board's insistence on running a tight ship and complying with strict financial controls began to be put to the test when the men making the financial recovery easier than it could have been started to question their rewards. The players were being sorted out one by one, but now the manager and his assistant were, quite reasonably, feeling hard done by. Not only were they performing miracles for peanuts but other clubs were taking notice. Keith had already expressed his amazement to Gary that his counterpart at struggling York City had just been awarded a three-year contract. He wasn't impressed by promises of pay rises next season either.

"We'd like to be paid a reasonable amount for what we've done, not what we're going to do next year." he said. "I've had one or two enquiries from other League clubs but my kids are at school here. I've been travelling to places like Ilkeston and Northwich for the last ten years or so and I'm quite happy in Lincolnshire. I don't want to leave, but I've got a young family and I can't work for next to nothing."

Cagey as ever, the board made one or two offers. They weren't trying to upset the men who were leading the recovery, but the majority of the directors were new to football and the financial near-death experience of the previous summer had made them very wary of spending money. There were people looking over their shoulders every time they did, too. However, they knew they'd got a star in their midst and it would be bad business to lose him, so eventually the deals were done.

With business behind the scenes resolved for now, the team kept picking up points and, whilst automatic promotion might have been a bridge too far, the play-offs were a distinct possibility. When asked by fans about the prospects of finishing in the top seven, Keith would use his by now well-known saying – "We'll be there or thereabouts". Again he enthused about the way his squad had responded to his demands.

"Probably the most pleasing aspect is the way I can see players improving game after game," he said. "A lot have come from non-league and we're talking Unibond here not Conference. That's a big jump to make."

"The gaffer doesn't really say much to us – win, lose, or draw," said captain Paul Morgan, giving a revealing insight into his manager's style. "And he certainly doesn't rant. He's very relaxed and that rubs off on all us players. If you're doing badly he reassures you at half-time and gives you a bit of confidence, which is great."

The chance of promotion was having an impact on Keith and Helen's social life too.

"We started going for a meal at the Farmer's Arms at Welton Hill on a Saturday night after a game," said Helen. "And, with the team doing well, we thought it might bring bad luck if we stopped our weekend routine. I think we ended up having everything on the menu at least twice by the end of the season."

The board were pleased with Keith and his team, there was a buzz around the club and the fans were more than happy. Some opposing managers were complimentary about Lincoln's work ethic and team spirit. One or two were less than enthusiastic, though, and made some 'lengthy' comments. Rob Newman of Southend complained about the long grass at Sincil Bank, suggesting it was to stop his side's passing football. Chris Turner had already objected to the number of long balls bombarding them. And Leroy Rosenior at Torquay had a dig at the long throws that were aimed at Lincoln's centre-halves who had pushed up into their penalty area. He might be laid back with his players, but Keith was starkly upright when it came to defending them.

"It's definitely a question of sour grapes. We're not getting any credit for the football we're playing," he fumed. "Everybody expects to beat us, home or away, without a challenge. Well those days are gone; we're not lying down for anybody. I like 4-4-2 but I don't have the players for that system on the wages we're paying with my next-to-nothing budget. We're playing on a pitch and using a formation, 5-3-2 or 5-2-3, that suits us, not the opposition. All I care about is my players and picking up points."

Lincoln did indeed keep picking up points and they kept their position in the top seven of the league too. As the season reached its climax, they travelled to the south coast for their penultimate game of the season against promotion rivals Bournemouth. Keith and Gary got their preparations and tactics spot-on as the Imps won 1-0, almost certainly ensuring a play-off place. By now, midfielder Richard Butcher was proving to be one of the best signings they'd made, with his surging runs from box to box and a significant contribution in the scoring stakes. His goal at Dean Court was one of the best, a strike from twenty five yards that the keeper never stood a chance of stopping.

Bournemouth had won at Sincil Bank in October, and another defeat by them would have meant Keith's team would need other clubs to help out when they played the final match at home to Torquay. As it turned out, what was probably their best performance of the season meant that a draw would be good enough the following Saturday.

In the week leading up to the game, Keith demonstrated his skill as a manager and how it might differ from some of his counterparts elsewhere. Chris Cornelly had suffered a serious injury and was on the long road to recovery. His contract was due to run out at the end of July. Keith gave the lad another year's deal, even though a long part of it would be spent recovering from his operation, let alone getting back to match fitness. The board was still looking to save money, despite the increase in attendances, and still trying to make sure what was spent got as much return as possible, so Keith was asked what would the club get from a player who would be sidelined for quite some time.

He was quick to point out that the player had a young wife and new baby. What message would it send to the rest of the squad if their manager put a lad on the scrapheap with a young family to care for and a mortgage to pay? He also said that the player was one who could turn a match our way in an instant, even if he was only likely to play a limited role later on next season. We didn't query the decision again.

Keith was equally blunt in his comments in the lead-up to the Torquay match. It was as if the more successful his young squad was, the more he wanted to defend them from their critics.

"I've reminded the players about our trip to Torquay when we battled for a point and were then slaughtered for it," he said defiantly. "The only way to answer the rants about us is to go out there on Saturday afternoon and win the game. We always go for a win – we don't score enough goals to go for a point – and if we get one, Torquay have to get two. That's how we must approach the game."

With results going badly for Lincoln elsewhere, they were one down for much of the match, and it could have been worse but for keeper Alan Marriott's penalty save. Striker Simon Yeo was still a cult hero with the home fans, despite a barren spell that had lasted months. Keith took off defender Simon Weaver and sent Yeo on and, after a couple of missed chances, he received a delightful through ball from Richard Butcher in the 86th minute and buried it with his left foot. The near capacity crowd went wild, Lincoln hung on, the final whistle blew, and Keith, Gary and their squad had reached the play-offs.

"I never went to games. Lincoln or anywhere. I didn't want to hear it if Keith got abuse shouted at him," said Helen. "But I went to the last game because I just had to be there. It was so tense, though. All I could do was sit in the executive lounge and listen to the crowd. Then there was a tremendous roar and Fran Martin burst in to confirm we'd equalised, and I was ecstatic."

Their opponents in the semifinal were old adversaries Scunthorpe. Their manager, Brian Laws, had joined the queue of those complaining about the Imps earlier in the season, by accusing Keith and Gary of being less than concerned about one of his players who had suffered a bad injury in a league game between the two clubs. Keith was more concerned about the team he was going to select and he knew there was a clamour for Yeo to start the game. Privately, he said he'd settle for a draw even though the first leg was at Sincil Bank. He thought his lads would relish the away game, soaking up pressure and attacking on the break. In terms of statistics, Lincoln hadn't scored a lot of goals over the season to reach the play-offs but they hadn't conceded a huge number either. Consequently, Keith and everyone else in the ground that day could hardly believe their eyes as his team ran out 5-3 winners in probably one of the most dramatic games ever seen at Sincil Bank.

Lincoln were 3-1 up but late on, Scunthorpe pulled it back to 3-3. Enter into the action Mr Yeo, who Keith had decided to keep on the subs bench, and who blasted two late goals to elevate his cult status to a level akin with Lincoln Cathedral and that infamous Imp. Apart from Brian Laws refusing to shake Keith's hand as they left the pitch, it was a great day for Lincoln's manager.

The away leg was no formality, despite the two-goal advantage. If Scunthorpe were to get an early goal, they would gain the initiative and anything could happen. The Yeo dilemma wasn't quite as difficult for Keith to solve because even the player knew that his side would have to contain their opponents and he would probably be on the bench again, ready and willing to come on if needed.

"I didn't mind being substitute, even for these important games," said Simon. "I'm just glad after all these years to be a professional footballer. The gaffer told me when I first came to always be at the back stick and I'll always get goals. That's good advice, and if I get on, I'll try and nick one."

In the last couple of minutes immediately before kick-off, something happened that illustrated how differently football managers try to impose themselves to get an advantage. Laws took it on himself to run around the Glanford Park pitch holding a Scunthorpe flag to raise the enthusiasm and volume of the home crowd still further. He even ran to the centre circle and planted the flag in the centre spot, before leaving the pitch and heading down the tunnel. Even if you'd offered Keith Alexander a whopping pay rise and the promise that his playing budget would be doubled, he would never have attempted such a stunt. That wasn't his style at all. He did, however, relate the incident to his players as they left the dressing room, and they needed no greater incentive to get a result.

Whilst the atmosphere was electric and the tension for everyone connected with the away club unbearable, the Lincoln team resorted to type and defended superbly, keeping their opponents at bay. Then late on, you-know-who came on as sub, received the ball on the halfway line and tore towards the Scunthorpe goal. He slipped the ball under the keeper to give the Imps an unassailable 6-3 lead and the 2,000 away fans behind that goal went crazy. For the first time in their history, Lincoln City had qualified to play at the national stadium, and they needed only one more win to gain promotion.

Brian Laws was magnanimous in defeat. "I've given my thoughts on what the dispute was about but I'm man enough to shake Keith's hand and congratulate him on reaching the final," he said, although he added that he thought Lincoln would struggle against fellow finalists Bournemouth at Cardiff.

"Brian knows that one or two things have gone off that shouldn't have done," said Keith. "I'm happy that he came and shook my hand."

In some ways, that quote was a measure of how Keith had developed as a manager and a communicator. He was fiercely protective of his players and he wouldn't tolerate them being criticised by other people. They weren't just his employees or members of his team. They were his footballing offspring. If they did what he asked, then he'd defend them if other people didn't like it. He was clearly good at getting on with people and he was always polite and friendly to fans, staff, and directors alike. It had been a roller coaster season but he'd been the one to make things happen and so it was him they all wanted to speak to, which he dutifully did.

When he came into board meetings, he put across his report succinctly, and patiently answered directors' questions, even when some of them made you cringe. He handled the media well and diffused their attempts at controversy. Once in an interview in his office, he was asked if he was disappointed with a player who'd been sent off for a reckless tackle. He replied by saying the only thing he was disappointed with was the quality of the fruit in the bowl on his desk, and he'd be taking that up with his wife.

Like a lot of managers, he was more at ease in the company of football people like other managers or former team-mates, but that hadn't stopped him developing a style of dealing with everyone else in a way that they liked and was fair. Even so, you sensed he was always watching for something to go against him. No doubt his first spell at Sincil Bank had something to do with that. And that was probably a very sensible approach, even though he was having some success the second time round. In football you should always remember you never know what's around the corner, however well things seem to be going at the time.

*****

And so to Cardiff and that play-off final. The build-up to the game included an already exhausted office staff selling thousands of tickets and laying on coaches for queues of fans, while Keith and his squad tried to prepare as normal. At the same time, though, they had to deal with out of the ordinary matters such as being measured for suits that were provided by a well-wisher and responding to countless media requests. The day before the game the squad, directors and staff and their partners set up base camp at the luxurious Celtic Manor Hotel in Newport, although, true to form when it came to spending money, only the rooms occupied by the manager, his staff and players were paid for by the club. In some ways, the opulent surroundings seemed a bit over the top after everyone involved with the club had spent the last ten months scrimping and saving. Keith soon reminded everyone they deserved it after all their hard work.

"The hotel was a good choice, because it made us all feel special," said Helen. "Although Gary never stopped complaining about how expensive the food was! There was a huge bottle of champagne behind the bar and Keith said he'd buy it for us all if we won. When they told him it was priced at £500, he changed his mind. It was a nice thought though."

Watching Keith and his team walk on to the pitch was an emotional moment but when the whistle blew and it was down to business, we hoped the occasion hadn't got to them and they would perform like they had all season. Sadly that wasn't the case. After a cagey first thirty minutes, Steve Fletcher volleyed in a Marcus Browning knock-down to put Bournemouth one up. Ben Futcher powered in a header from a corner a few minutes later to equalise, but Carl Fletcher headed a goal in first-half stoppage time to restore their lead. In the second half, Lincoln's defence was uncharacteristically disorganised and allowed Stephen Purches and then Garreth O'Connor to extend their lead. Mark Bailey gave us some hope when he headed in with a quarter of an hour left, but only a minute later the defence was nowhere as Carl Fletcher made it 5-2 with his second goal of the game, doubling his goal tally for the season. Over the 90 minutes the Poppies created about six chances and took five of them. We seemed to have twice as many efforts on goal, didn't convert them, and lost heavily.

"We're disappointed but we've had a tremendous season. I've had a good day out and I've got myself a new suit," said Keith. "This time last year we hadn't been paid for eight weeks and now we've just had a couple of days in the Celtic Manor Hotel. We came here to win but we were beaten by a better team. I think we contributed to it by producing probably our worst defensive display of the season. We gave away sloppy goals against a team that seemed to score every time they had a shot. The scoreline might suggest we were overawed by the occasion but I don't think it got to the players. We were just poor on the day. I don't know why we defended so badly."

Even though the season had ended in disappointment and the action was finally over, Keith continued to show both his managerial strength and his personal pride by keeping the players on the pitch as Bournemouth collected their medals.

"After the final whistle I told the players to get up. We weren't going to sit around crying," he said. "We'd played as well as we could on the day. All right, we could have defended better, but they had beaten us and it was a matter of showing respect to them and to our fans who had come to Cardiff and didn't want to see us slope off down the tunnel. What would the fans have done if we had? They would have sloped off too rather than stayed behind. We had to stand up and be strong. Emotional though the game is, I didn't want the players feeling sorry for themselves. It was time to be mentally tough."

The following Monday was a bank holiday and, before the final, the local council had suggested the club had an open-top bus ride up to the Guildhall where they would host a civic reception. Some of us thought that this was a bit over the top after losing the game 5-2. As usual, Keith's common sense approach shone through.

"I was also in two minds whether to cancel the parade," he said. "I certainly didn't think it was a good idea on Saturday night, and Sunday too, because we hadn't won anything. But then I just thought that a lot of people would be expecting us to turn up and would it be right for us to spoil their bit of pleasure?"

It turned out to be a wise decision. Thousands lined the route and, while the mayor of Lincoln greeted the squad and officials high within the historic Guildhall, supporters outside chanted for Keith and the players. The second the formalities were over, he left his seat and threw open the windows so that he, his captain and his team-mates could, one by one, shout their thanks down to the sea of red and white below, who roared their approval.

This moment went some way to answering a question that had puzzled a lot of us. It seemed crazy to think that after almost ten months of sweat and toil by everyone connected with Lincoln City, losing the final didn't matter. No-one with any pride or ambition would openly admit it, surely. But the club nearly went under, and when it survived by the skin of its teeth, the team were everyone's first choice to finish bottom. Keith had led the way in proving them wrong and, such was the promise his charges had shown, it was felt they could maybe go one better next time. Of course we'd have loved to have gone up, but there had been so much gained anyway. The League Managers Association also agreed that falling at the final hurdle didn't reduce the impact Keith had made, when they presented him with an award at their end-of-season dinner. Typically, he said the prize was down to his players.

"The team have come on leaps and bounds in the short time they've been together and they're a year ahead of schedule," he said. "Expectations grew as the team improved. Our first target was fifty points, then sixty, and then seventy which got us into the play-offs. I'll always remember two or three things about the season – the reaction to Simon Yeo's equaliser against Torquay and walking out of the tunnel at the Millennium Stadium to see all our fans and hear them singing. Then back in Lincoln, seeing all those people along the High Street and in front of the Guildhall and generally just watching the players grow and people come back to a club that was almost dead a year ago. Next year we're going for automatic promotion and if we don't make it, we'll be disappointed not to finish in the top seven."

Keith Alexander might always remember a few things, but a lot of people would remember a great many things about a man who led their club from near oblivion to the promise of a very bright future. In his first full season back as a Football League manager, his eventful career as a player and non-league boss had been a good basis for him to develop his skills so quickly. That season would also go some way to prepare him for the highs and lows that were to follow.

2

Childhood, Starting Out, Scoring at Wembley

"I used to say to the players 'just give him the ball'"
Malcolm Hird

Keith Alexander was born in Nottingham on 14th November, 1956. John and Josie, his parents, had moved to England from St Lucia along with thousands of others who made their way here from colonial countries in the post-war economic boom and to help resolve severe labour shortages. They settled in the East Midlands where they worked and brought up Keith, his brothers Randall, Delroy and Kentry, and his sister Nova. At the age of two, Keith was diagnosed as having genu varum, or bow-leggedness. Although this is common in children under eighteen months, as young legs gradually straighten from the position they held in the womb, doctors in those days preferred to act if this took longer. As a result, they decided Keith should wear steel and leather leg braces for the next twelve months.

Sport, and in particular football, played a big part in the life of each member of the Alexander family. They voraciously watched it on TV and when Keith was four, John, deciding the lad was old enough, took him for the first of many visits to the City Ground to see Nottingham Forest play. In the late '50s and early '60s, Forest took over from Notts County as the biggest club in the city. Despite losing Ray Dwight, uncle of Elton John, with a broken leg, they won the FA Cup in 1959 and became a formidable side in the First Division. County, meanwhile, slipped down the leagues, finishing bottom of the Third Division in 1964.

This was the era of Harold Wilson, John F Kennedy, The Beatles, the Great Train Robbery and Spurs winning the League and FA Cup double. They were exciting times for an energetic and athletic young boy living in Mapperley and he spent every spare moment playing football in the local parks and on the local pitches with his brothers and pals.

At around the same time as England won the World Cup in 1966, Keith Alexander captained the Elms Junior School football team. His class teacher, Paul Ritchie, coached the team and played Keith out on the right wing. Paul described his captain as a 'super footballer' and his faith in him was justified when he was selected for Nottingham City Schools Under 11s. An equally promising Viv Anderson, later to play for Forest and become the first black footballer to represent England, played alongside Keith in the same team. A young boy called Alan Parker played against Keith in those early school years but they found themselves on the same side when they both moved up to Manvers Pierrepont Comprehensive School on Carlton Road. Not only did they become team-mates but they hit it off and were firm friends for many years.

"We both played for the school team," recalled Alan. "I got to know Keith really well and I was always knocking about with him. I nearly lived at his house on Corby Road, I was with him that often. Keith was much taller than all the other kids. He wore number ten and was a natural goal-scorer. Mind you, he was a lazy bugger to begin with. He expected us to win the ball and give him it. Then he'd beat about five players in his languid style and lay on a chance or, more often that not, score himself."

The two friends joined Clifton All-Whites, a Sunday youth league team that was largely made up of young lads from the Clifton area of Nottingham. The team comprised a lot of talented players like Pedro Richards who went on to make nearly 400 appearances for Notts County.

"We generally won at least one trophy a season," said Parker. "Keith was well liked at school and, when he started playing youth football, he became a very popular young lad around Nottingham. He had no aggression in him at all and was always well behaved."

The Parker and Alexander partnership was maintained when, as fifteen-year-olds, they joined Clifton Rangers. For a bit of variety Keith played a lot of local cricket and was a handy batsman for Old Paviors Cricket Club.

In the late '60s and early '70s life wasn't without its challenges for a large black family living in Nottingham. Keith used to volunteer to run errands for people who lived nearby to earn a few shillings. A busy local hairdresser was happy to recruit him and, realising she was out of dog food, asked him to go to the corner shop for her. Keith stood at the counter and politely told the assistant what he wanted as he placed payment down on the counter. "Yes, they tell me you lot like it in a stew," she said quietly under her breath as she reached up and grasped the tin from the shelf above her. Her comment wasn't quiet enough for her customer not to have heard it, though, and Keith's heart sank as he left the shop and realised what she'd meant.

Whilst racism was abhorred by most right-thinking people around that time, just as much as it is now, the media had a funny way of showing it. The BBC's hit sit-com *Till Death Us Do Part* featured cockney character and West Ham fan Alf Garnett spouting his racist and anti-socialist views. Clearly these views were so extreme and so unacceptable they were humorous to those who appreciated the satirical thrust of the programme.

However, there must have been other less insightful viewers who didn't appreciate the comedic tactic being employed and who enjoyed his ranting and raving. "It stands to reason," he would say, before making a patently unreasonable comment about 'coons' or 'the Jews up at Spurs'. This was followed by *Love Thy Neighbour*, on ITV. Character Eddie Booth struggled to come to terms with the arrival of a black couple next door and this represented a metaphor for Britain's difficulties in coping with newly arrived immigrants. 'Nig-nog' and 'Sambo' were used instead of his neighbour's name, and it was small wonder that racism reared its ugly head in Nottingham and towns and cities up and down the country.

A less than humorous racist event was to affect the Alexander family during Keith's childhood. He stood and listened as his father opened the front door to a police officer who told them the family shop they were running at the time had been burned down. He said he believed it to be a racist attack and, despite investigations, the culprit was never found. The shop had been doing well and it took a long time for John and Josie to recover financially.

As a young man, Keith had a brief spell playing for a Sunday team in Nottingham that comprised only local black players. It was a standing 'joke' among the other clubs in their league, regrettably repeated many times, that playing against them in August or September was always harder than in December or January when it was supposedly too cold for them.

For all the difficulties he might have met, Keith enjoyed a happy childhood. His family life was busy, noisy, and there was a lot of fun and banter among the four brothers who all loved sport. He soon realised, though, that he'd be the person who would decide his destiny, no-one else, and if hard work was what it took to succeed, then work hard is what he'd do. He also decided that his two passions, family and football, would be his way of taking life by the throat and those passions would never waver.

*****

As a teenager, Keith was practical and good with his hands. He could be relied on when it came to DIY jobs around the house. He left school at sixteen and was taken on as an apprentice joiner at Boots shopfitters on Carlton Boulevard in Nottingham where he combined learning a trade with playing football locally. He played in Mapperley in the same team as Kentry and Randolph and he signed for Corby Road Rovers for a season. Keith began to make good friends in the area through his involvement in local football and, when he went to Germany for a brief spell on a building contract, he was quick to return, missing his family and football friends. One of these was Tony Downie, who he met when they both played for Clifton All-Whites. Ironically the club name was subsequently changed to Clifton Town as requested by the local FA, for politically correct reasons. Tony and Keith had played against each other for their schools and they enjoyed going out in Nottingham together when they were considered old enough to do so by their families. Keith suffered a broken leg in a youth team game, but when it had healed he was delighted to sign amateur forms for Notts County when he was eighteen.

Whilst his experience at Meadow Lane was useful, all Keith wanted to do was play, and play as much as possible. Consequently he had no hesitation in moving from club to club. It was as if he wanted to meet as many players, coaches and managers as possible and learn from them all. As a nineteen and twenty-year-old, his whirlwind tour of local teams took in Wisbech, Arnold Town, Worksop Town, Clifton, Attenborough, Kimberley Town and Alfreton Town. Then he and Tony signed for Ilkeston Town in the 1977-78 season, with Keith making his debut in the home game against Louth United in September. He played seventeen games and scored once. Working long hours in the building trade, socialising, training, and playing football weren't enough so he also qualified as a referee. One thing was for sure, no-one could ever accuse Keith Alexander of idling his time away.

*****

When Tony Downie and his brother Clyde signed for Stamford,

nicknamed the Daniels, of the United Counties League, during the 1978-79 season, they were quick to recommend Keith to manager Ray Medwell. Although this was clearly Stamford's gain, they were later to admit their generous testimonial was mainly because the south Lincolnshire town was a long way from Nottingham, and tired of catching buses and cadging lifts, they knew their pal had a car and their travelling problems would be solved. Medwell's good friend and former Stamford stalwart Malcolm Hird had been recruited as his assistant and both of them realised that Keith was a very good signing, the manager employing him as a left-back. Although good mates, as the season developed the management duo didn't gel and Hird decided to stand down. When Medwell was sacked in the close season, the board asked Hird to return and take over.

At his first training session, the new manager had only nine players standing there listening to his plans for the new season. The budget was very low so he went about signing local lads instead of established players, but he made sure they were big, strong and mobile. He wanted to put together a close-knit team who would compete against sides who were stronger on paper. Keith fitted the bill perfectly and as a gangly 6' 4" youngster with a lot of skill, Hird knew he was wasted playing at the back and would do a good job further up the field.

Despite the low expectations of the Stamford fans, their team won their first nine games. Keith played up front and although often appearing awkward, could beat one opponent after another or hold the ball up with ease. His team-mates often thought he'd lost control of the ball, only for it to suddenly look like it was Velcro-ed to one boot or other once more. Defenders who weren't particularly taller but were much wider tried in vain to knock him off the ball and, although skinny, he gave as good as he got.

"I just used to say 'give him the ball.' In fact I told all the players they should never stop giving him it," said Hird.

"Keith was very influential with his skill and he was a match winner, either with the goals he scored or the ones he set up."

As the wins kept coming, one or two equally talented players came on board to strengthen the squad still further. Some travelled fairly long distances like Keith, now living in Boston, or goalkeeper Kevin Johnson from Holbeach, but such was the spirit among the team, they never missed training. Keith became firm friends with Hird and he often called at his house for tea before they went off to their training session that night. Keith had married his long-term girlfriend, Val, by now and the two of them often went for a night out with Malcolm and his wife, Linda. The squad were all very close and many times all of them and their wives and partners enjoyed a night out together in Stamford after a game.

Sitting at the top of the league was beyond most people's expectations, but then the UCL Knockout Cup and FA Vase came along and Stamford did well in those too. It certainly wasn't a case of getting them out the way and concentrating on the league. In the FA Vase, after drawing at Soham Town Rangers and winning the replay, they beat Letchworth Garden City of the Isthmian League and won 3-2 at county rivals Skegness Town who plied their trade in the Midland League. Then they knocked out the previous year's semifinalists Shepshed Charterhouse. Stamford, whilst still clocking up points in their pursuit of the league title, also started to dream of a Wembley appearance. Two wins later, at home to Desborough Town and away at Cray Wanderers, and the Daniels were in the two-legged semifinal against Curzon Ashton.

Used as a striker or on the left side of midfield, Keith was playing well and he had reached double figures by now, as well as setting up probably three times as many goals for his team-mates. In the home leg against Curzon Ashton he scored the second in a 2-0 win, and he made sure his side were in the final by getting both in another 2-0 victory at their place. Little Stamford were at Wembley to play Guisborough Town and the whole town was in raptures.

Manager Malcolm Hird had played in the FA Vase final when his team had lost 1-0 to Billericay in 1976. All he could remember was that Stamford's opponents had been thoroughly professional in how they dealt with the match and the occasion. This seemed to give them a head start and he insisted his side should do the same. The team had already had one or two overnight stays on the way to the final and they travelled to London on the Friday before the game, staying in the Europa Hotel near the stadium. The players were seen off by a huge crowd of fans in the centre of Stamford, and, Hird having worked on a couple of enthusiastic sponsors, the squad had been provided with jumpers with 'Wembley 1980' embroidered on them for the journey. They also had matching blazers, trousers, shirts and ties for the day itself.

On the Friday night, Keith and some of the players couldn't contain their curiosity, so they paid to get into Wembley alongside the punters heading for the dog racing inside the stadium. Ignoring the greyhounds hurling themselves around the track, they took in the size of the place and had a good look at that famous pitch. They only stayed a short time and wandered back to the hotel feeling much better about the day ahead.

The following morning, thousands of Stamford fans set off for the final in a convoy of coaches. The squad wanted to follow the same routine that had got them there, so they found a park near the hotel and did some light training. Those Stamford fans gave their team a tremendous reception as they walked out on to the pitch in a special change strip of yellow shirts, blue shorts, and yellow socks. The game was tight and tense as expected but in the first half Keith settled everyone's nerves by being first to a cross and sliding the ball home from close range. Then Andy McGowan got a second and, although Guisborough rallied and put the Daniels under extreme pressure in the second half, Stamford held firm and the cup was theirs.

Carlsberg, the sponsors, had put on a posh do for the teams and their families but, as close-knit as ever, Stamford made a brief appearance, made their apologies and left. They were desperate to get home and celebrate their triumph with everyone in Stamford – families, friends and fans. They all congregated at the Danish Invader pub in the town and the place was rocking until the early hours for most, and the next morning for quite a few. Weeks later, the club totted up the proceeds of their Wembley success and the contractors moved in to install floodlights at the ground for the first time. Everyone connected with the Daniels might know how to celebrate but they also knew how to spend money wisely, especially when it would help their club grow and increase their chances of advancing up the football pyramid.

Hird was delighted at his team's success in winning their league and two cup competitions, but he also felt a tinge of regret. He suspected his star striker and good friend would think he'd reached another crossroads. Whether a team had done well or done badly, he could see the advantage in moving on, and the lure of another club might prove too much of a temptation for Keith Alexander.

3

Around the Grounds, Never a Dull Moment at Underhill

"I honestly thought they were going to lynch him at the end"
Keith Rudd

Malcolm Hird was right and, despite the success Keith had enjoyed at Stamford, the footballing wanderlust struck again. It didn't matter if his current club's prospects were good or not so good; a new challenge and new faces always seemed to appeal to Keith. He was good at making friends too, so arriving at another club held no fears for him. When he'd leave, many of these friends remained close for years to come.

Keith next decided to accept the offer to sign for his then home town club, Boston United, but he only made a handful of appearances for the first team. The Pilgrims were in the Alliance Premier League and this higher standard of football meant that Keith found his chances limited. Secretary John Blackwell became another close pal and Keith often called in at the club after work for a chat and a cuppa. Despite not playing as often as he'd hoped, he felt comfortable at York Street and he'd sometimes describe some of his ambitions in football.

"Keith was often here because he lived in Boston and we became good mates," said John. "He was only a young man but you could tell he was already thinking about his future in football. He was very level-headed. I know it sounds strange but we could already see he'd be the sort who would stay in the game a long time, probably as a manager. I often thought he'd maybe be a good manager for us one day."

Keen to play some games, Keith was loaned out to Kings Lynn where he made a dozen appearances and scored three goals, including the winner at Morecambe. Again, he was in and out the team, so, having been told one Friday he'd be substitute the following day, he reported that he was injured and turned out for Bourne Town instead. He might have been a bit lax when it came to rules and regulations but, because Keith was such a likeable lad, no-one at Kings Lynn minded when it came to light that he'd decided to add another club to the already long list he'd represented.

Another football rule, or at least an unwritten one, is never go back. Needless to say, Keith ignored this convention when the offer to return to Stamford was put to him at the start of the 1981-82 season. He enjoyed another full season for the Daniels, whose nickname arose long ago when, for reasons known only to those at the time, the team were named after Daniel Lambert. Daniel's claim to fame was that he was the fattest man in Britain, and when he died they had to take a wall down at his house to remove his fifty-two stone body.

Keith and Val celebrated the birth of their first son, Matthew, in September and, the following May, Stamford celebrated another United Counties League and Knockout Cup double. Keith scored eleven goals in his forty-three appearances and, although success in the FA Vase had eluded them this time, it had been another tremendous season for both the player and the club.

Another change loomed when Malcolm Hird, now managing Corby Town, gave Keith a ring. Keith was pleased to join up with his old boss but, on his debut, soon realised that the friendly atmosphere at Stamford was a thing of the past. Fighting broke out between opposing players at every opportunity and Malcolm was so disgusted that he resigned twenty minutes after the game. Their reunion had therefore turned out to be very brief. Keith lasted one more game before following suit, upping sticks and signing for Spalding, where he scored a creditable eighteen goals in thirty seven Northern Counties East League games. In a match against Skegness, John Cockerill played against him and they enjoyed a beer and a few laughs together after the final whistle. They instantly hit it off and were to become firm friends.

Keith added to his growing collection of Lincolnshire clubs by having brief spells at Boston Town and at Grantham where he played alongside Cockerill. The two of them then swapped their Lincolnshire loyalty for Norfolk, joining Kings Lynn for the second half of the 1983-84 season. Manager Keith Rudd was pleased to have persuaded Keith to have a second spell with the Linnets, although he often joked afterwards that he had signed the big striker for a promotion push and they hardly won a game after he arrived.

Keith made his debut in December away at Welling who had a young Andy Townsend, later to star for Chelsea, Aston Villa, and the Republic of Ireland, playing impressively for them in midfield. Kings Lynn won 2-1 to remain top of the league. The manager remembered his new player as a bit of a lad in his first spell, often getting into scrapes. His view of Keith second time round was quite different.

"We used to talk about the game for hours," said Rudd. "I used to tell him to think football all the time and it seemed to rub off. He was like a student of the game, taking everything in. And he always had ambitions to go higher and play at a better level. He'd had years working and playing and he knew what a great life full-time professionals had."

Keith Rudd could see that Keith Alexander had changed in some ways but had also retained a lot of his pleasing characteristics.

"He was as laid back as when he was here the first time. He would infuriate me," said Rudd. "He'd beat four men and then run the ball into touch. Other times his ability with the ball destroyed the opposition. But he never got angry. I used to shout to him 'Keith, for Christ's sake – get bloody nasty!' and he'd just look across at me grinning."

In a top-of-the-table clash at Fisher Athletic in south-east London, the away team were on the receiving end of some very robust tactics. Keith tormented them by keeping possession as the tackles came flying in. Several times he was sent crashing to the ground and most of the time it was because he'd been fouled. Whether the referee had given a free-kick or not, each time Keith picked himself up and smiled at his opponents before regaining possession of the ball and running at them. In the last minute, with the score at 2-2, Les McJannet crossed for Keith to head in the winner. Just as the referee was about to blow for time, Lynn player Marty Wiles was felled by a punch and the offending Fisher player was sent off. A mass brawl ensued and it seemed all the home players were trying to get at Keith Alexander. He kept out of the way and, even then, dealt with the situation by smiling and keeping calm.

"He had immense self-control," confirmed Rudd. "Fisher tried every trick in the book to stop us playing and to stop Keith running the show. He got horrendous abuse from the fans. I honestly thought they were going to lynch him at the end. And all he'd done was give them a football lesson."

After celebrating the birth of his second son, Paul, in the spring of 1984, Keith, now aged twenty-seven, was contacted by Dave Needham. If it took a Nottingham connection to persuade him to leave Kings Lynn, then Needham was the man. A giant of a centre-half, he'd played for Notts County for eleven years and, after a very brief sojourn in the capital with Queens Park Rangers, had enjoyed another five years with Forest. He had recognised that Keith was capable at playing at a higher level and, as manager of Kettering Town, was delighted to sign him up for the 1984-85 season. The Poppies competed in the GM Vauxhall Conference, one step below the Football League, but Keith was now a mature young man and he'd worked out what he needed to do to play well alongside and against better players.

He made his debut in the final of the pre-season Maunsell Cup competition against Peterborough United. Kettering won

4-2 on penalties after a 1-1 draw and Keith did enough to earn a place in the team as the league campaign got under way. He made his debut against Altrincham and scored his first goal for his new club against Bath City in early September. He was a regular in the side and, when they won four games in a row, including a 4-0 thumping of Barnet to go fourth in the table in the New Year, the Kettering fans dreamt that their team and their exciting new striker could win the title for them. Sadly, only three more wins in the remaining games meant that those hopes were dashed, but finishing halfway in a strong league was still considered a creditable achievement.

Keith had played regularly, done well and his distinctive style was getting him noticed. Needham managed to get him to sign up for another season but promised he wouldn't stand in his way if a good offer came along. Keith appreciated this and also recognised that the team had been strengthened in certain areas so he could, for once, see the sense in staying put. Again, he was a regular in the team as Kettering, competing in a bizarre new points system where a home win was rewarded with two points and an away victory with three, amassed enough of them in total to finish an impressive ninth in the table.

As the campaign began to draw to a close, the offers did indeed come along. Knowing that his player was unlikely to agree to another season at Rockingham Road, Needham agreed to let him go out on loan to Wisbech Town. They were having a great run in the FA Vase, so Keith was more than happy to join them and have another chance of playing at Wembley before he accepted the best offer on the table for the 1986-87 season. Manager Roy McManus was convinced that his new recruit would be the final ingredient in going all the way in the cup, and when Keith scored a hat-trick on his debut in a 5-0 win at Harwich, McManus was delighted he'd been able to bolster an already good team at just the right time.

In the semifinal at Southall in front of a big crowd, Keith

was impressive and scored one of the goals in a 2-2 draw. An even bigger crowd at Fenland Park expected Wisbech to complete the task in the second leg, but the home fans were sadly disappointed when a youthful Les Ferdinand, a future Premier League player and England international, scored both goals as Southall won 2-0 to go through 4-2 on aggregate.

*****

Playing in the lower leagues, often for well-run clubs in quiet rural locations, had served Keith Alexander well. He'd experienced a range of managerial styles and represented teams who battled away physically or had tried to play attractive football. Some had attempted a combination of the two. He'd learned a lot and in the summer of 1986 he was set to learn a whole lot more. The coming season would see the champions of the GM Vauxhall Conference rewarded with automatic promotion to the Football League for the first time. For years, successful non-league clubs hoped that the re-election system would abandon its old pals act of preserving the league status of clubs that had finished bottom of the pile, but it rarely happened.

As a result of the rule change, chairmen and managers suddenly became much more ambitious. This ambition would manifest itself in players being paid more and being urged to be more ruthless. Playing for fun for a few quid to supplement the earnings from the day job began to be a thing of the past. After considering a few decent offers, Keith accepted the one Barnet had put in front of him. Playing in London after appearing for all those country town clubs wouldn't be the only difference he'd experience by going to Underhill.

Chairman Stan Flashman, born in East London, had bought the club for £50,000 in 1985. He made his money as a high-profile ticket tout and if you wanted tickets for the final on the Centre Court at Wimbledon or a royal garden party, then Stan was your man. It was rumoured he'd even sold someone an invitation to Princess Anne's wedding. His manager was Barry Fry, who was back at Barnet after a brief spell at Maidstone United, and was well known as a larger-than-life character and for his wheeling and dealing. Flashman and Fry were to develop a turbulent working relationship, the like of which Keith had never experienced before. The pair were best of friends one minute and at each other's throats the next, with the players never knowing what to expect from them – especially when it came to their manager being given the boot.

It was widely reported that Fry was sacked and then re-instated at least eight times. However, the manager was to report years later, possibly with a little bit of characteristic exaggeration, that he'd been dismissed thirty-seven times during his time at Underhill. Flashman's attempts to interfere in team affairs were also well known, along with Fry's resistance to it. He once told 'Fat Stan' that he "didn't know a goal-line from a fucking washing line" which probably only made things worse.

Fry was prolific in the transfer market; a strategy that was to stay with him throughout his managerial career. One chairman was quoted as saying that he thought his manager was trying to solve the nation's unemployment problem single-handed. Fry, now Director of Football at Peterborough United, was good at spotting talent though, and he was happy he'd persuaded Keith to move from Kettering.

"When I lived in Bedford, I used to watch Kettering a fair bit. I fancied Keith for Barnet from what I saw there," said Fry. "He'd got great skill and was good at holding the ball up."

Keith was excited by the challenge of being at a club that was ambitious and wanted to get into the Football League. He was also impressed by his new manager's enthusiasm for the game. Keith was now working as a construction training officer in Spalding and that, combined with the decent money he would get from Barnet, was another plus.

Fry insisted his team would play an attacking brand of football. Keith joined Dave Sansom and Nicky Evans as a three-man strike force, but these gung-ho tactics meant that they often left gaping holes at the back and conceded as many as they scored. Nevertheless, Barnet were unbeaten, winning six and drawing five from the beginning of September to the end of October, and sat proudly at the top of the league.

The fans loved the cavalier football their team played. Keith became a cult hero and the youngsters standing on the old South Terrace adored him. As with any team doing well, there was huge competition for places in the starting line-up and Keith was sometimes a substitute as others got their chance. He preferred, instead of stretching and jogging along the touchline, to lean on the pitch-side railing out of his manager's view and chat to the home supporters.

One young fan, particularly taken by Keith's easy going nature, wrote to him via the club to ask for a signed photo. Late one evening at home with his parents, the lad heard the doorbell ring. His mother nervously opened the door just enough to see a very tall well-built stranger standing there asking if her son was in. The fan, dressed in his pyjamas, went to the door to be greeted by Keith Alexander, who thanked him for his letter and handed over a photo of the Barnet squad signed by every single player. He then smiled, strode off down the path turning to wave his farewell, and was gone.

In the second half of the season, Fry made what he was later to admit was an error that probably cost his team the title. He had two good keepers in his squad and he allowed Kevin Blackwell to leave. Blackwell signed for Scarborough, who were managed by Neil Warnock, and at that time were only around halfway in the table. Blackwell grasped the opportunity of regular first team action and was in inspired form as his new team went on an amazing run. Despite losing only three games between Xmas and the end of the season and with Keith scoring important goals and setting up others, Barnet were pipped to top spot by their Yorkshire rivals by two points.

Fry and his team were devastated but they resolved to make sure they wouldn't be so generous next time round. The manager was pleased to recruit Keith for another season and was full of praise for him.

"He was great to have around," enthused Fry. "He was a great thinker about the game, a good captain, and was always trying to better himself. He started doing some coaching for us and taking his badges, even though he knew he was very much an important part of the playing squad."

If the previous season had seen a more competitive edge creep into the highest echelon of the non-league scene, then the 1987-88 season was even more combative. Lincoln City had become the first club to suffer automatic relegation from the Football League and, hurt by that, they resolved to keep on a full-time playing staff in their efforts to get back. Conference clubs all had part-time players and resented Lincoln's decision, believing that this was against the spirit of their league. The debate was not lost on Keith either and, now aged thirty, he was worried he would never make the grade as a full-time player. He consoled himself that winning the league with Barnet would solve the problem, because a promoted club would need a squad of players who would devote all their time to winning games. After just missing out on promotion last time, they were firm favourites too.

Lincoln also resented the first couple of fixtures they'd been given as the season got underway. They felt they had been set up as sacrificial lambs when they were sent to Underhill as a sort of reward for last season's runners-up, and then to Weymouth to help the home club celebrate their first game in their brand new ground. Lincoln were soundly beaten in both games and, finding that everyone wanted to beat the former League club, manager Colin Murphy decided they would fight fire with fire.

Keith was a regular in the Barnet side and, if he wasn't scoring, he was creating chances for others. Because of this,

Barnet quickly found themselves top of the table and, after their dodgy start, Lincoln City were their main challengers from around October onwards. If the race to win the title had become a war, then the top-of-the-table clash between the two clubs at Sincil Bank was the battle, almost literally, that defined it.

"They were a nasty bunch. The game at their place was an awful experience," Barnet player Kevin Millett was reported as saying. "Our coach had to have a police escort to the ground, the dressing room floor was two inches deep in water and the warm-up balls they gave us were caked in mud. The crowd was really hostile and at half-time we heard that our fans were being given a hard time. The ref was appalling and we went down to nine men when Noel Ashford and Herbie Smith were sent off. Herbie and Keith were racially abused from the minute they stepped out on to the pitch. Small wonder we got beat."

Barnet put the defeat behind them and maintained their postion at the top. On Boxing Day they beat Enfield 3-0 with Keith scoring twice. Two days later he netted a hat-trick in a 6-2 win over Sutton United.

Despite playing at the highest level of his career, Keith's nomadic will to go wherever he fancied still hadn't left him. Maybe being part of a serious promotion campaign persuaded him that he wanted some fun too, or maybe it was easier to agree to someone's persuasive powers than let them down. Whatever the reason, Keith was hauled over the coals and fined two weeks wages by Barry Fry when he found out he'd appeared several times for a Sunday league team in Lincoln when he should have been at home resting after a vital game the day before.

Naturally, Fry would have had good cause to be angry if his star man had become unavailable by being injured in an over-zealous challenge by a pub-team opponent. But Keith was a rebel – not a serious rebel, but a rebel nonetheless. He couldn't see the point in not doing what he wanted to, if doing it was to him, no big deal. He would never hurt anyone and he would always do what was asked of him. He always saw the other person's point of view.

But he'd learned long ago that toeing the line and slavishly following the rules wasn't always the way to go, especially if he couldn't see much harm in a bit of rule-bending. And if his misdemeanour was detected, the person who had to tell him off usually did so by acting suitably seriously and afterwards quietly smiling to themselves because they couldn't help liking the guilty man. Not so much rebel without a cause as rebel without an edge.

In April, Barnet played at York Street, home of Boston United. Lincoln City were without a game and a lot of Imps fans, including myself and a couple of mates, went along to, for once, cheer on our near neighbours. If Barnet were to slip up, then Lincoln might just be able to take advantage. Fry selected Mark Flashman, the chairman's son, to play in goal. Whether he was good enough for this honour or his appearance was only down to the chairman's orders, we shall never know, but he struggled and Barnet suffered their first defeat in weeks. Of the three sets of fans in the ground, two were jubilant and one was very unhappy.

Inevitably, and in keeping with the season in general, a lot of ill-feeling and nastiness was the end result. The police and stewards struggled to keep control. Near us, Keith's team-mate Ed Stein was heard to try and calm down an especially abusive group of supporters and, in true non-league fashion, entered into a dialogue with them. I couldn't hear everything that was said but I couldn't miss the genuine look of dismay on Stein's face when the conversation ended by someone shouting "Yeah...well at least I'm not fucking black."

The last two rounds of Conference fixtures took place over the May Bank Holiday weekend. Keith knew that if his team performed anywhere near the way they'd played over the whole season, they'd do it. They were up against lowly opposition and, if they won both games, they would be champions and reach the promised land. In an interview live on television before their game against Runcorn, Fry was asked if his team would triumph. He made a recommendation that to most would seem pretty drastic, but to him was characteristically routine when it came to how to back a football club. He said the viewers should "put their house on it". Sometimes bravado is just destined to fail, and when Keith and his fellow strikers bombarded the Runcorn goal at Underhill without success, after the away side had taken an undeserved lead, the league title was out of their hands. Lincoln won to go top for the first time that season, and they won again on the Monday to regain their place in the Football League after just one season. The dream was over for Barnet and for Keith.

*****

In his travels around the non-league scene, Keith had learned a lot about playing the game, tactics, coaching, styles of play, and the different ways teams could get results. He'd learned how managers manage players, and people in general too, and win them over. And it some cases, how not to. Now, aged thirty-one, he needed to think about his career after playing. He wanted to stay in the game and develop players and construct winning sides. But he hadn't played full-time professional football, something he had always passionately wanted to do. Because of this, he knew he'd always be looked down on when it came to getting a coaching or managing job. For years, Keith had thought about the game and taken it all in. So he was never going to let anyone think he wasn't good enough because he hadn't been a pro-footballer. All he needed was one little break to make it happen.

4

Success on the Humber, Harry the Haddock, Early Days at Lincoln

"He was sitting in a bright orange Ford Capri looking out the window grinning and he'd got a huge afro haircut"
Grant Brown

Alan Buckley was a purist. He thought there was only one way to play the game. On the deck, pass and move, give and go. He was a striker too, or a former one, and he knew what he wanted when it came to building a team that played his way and created chances. He knew that some managers signed finishers and expected the midfield to set them up with crosses and through balls and they'd do the rest. Easy. Except it took more than that.

He hadn't scored a huge number of goals for Walsall and a host of other clubs at a rate of almost one every other game without working out that a striker needed to hold the ball up and bring others into the game. Then, with bodies supporting him, there would be more opportunities to be in the right place to whack a cross into the back of the net or latch on to a ball played through the defence and slide it home.

Buckley cut his teeth as a manager at Kettering from 1986 to 1988, and he'd impressed. They played good football and had a taste of success by winning the GMAC Cup, the non-league version of the League Cup. Grimsby Town recognised his potential and in June 1988, after two disastrous seasons that had seen consecutive relegations, they persuaded him to take over at Blundell Park.

Moving to a Football League club suited his ambitions as a manager. Having done his homework, Buckley joined them only on condition he was allowed to sign several players. He told the board that he needed at least half a dozen if they wanted success. If they backed him, they'd get it with a team that played in a way that put smiles back on their faces and, more importantly, back on the fans' faces too. That summer he signed six players, including John Cockerill from Stafford Rangers. Knowing he needed a striker who could create as many chances as he converted, he also gave Keith Alexander a ring.

Keith was delighted to get the call. Missing out on promotion with Barnet had been a big blow. After losing out on that precious chance to play in the Football League to a team from his home county, the irony of another one from Lincolnshire offering him that very chance was not lost on him. However, his eager anticipation at meeting Buckley and doing the deal was tinged a little bit with worry. Now thirty one, Keith was concerned he might only be given a short-term contract because of his age. He was even more worried that, when the chips were down and the manager knew everything about him, he might not get one at all. After a great deal of thought, coupled with a bottle of correction fluid and a photocopier, the problem was solved. With his date of birth carefully changed from 1956 to 1958 on his birth certificate, the deal was done with Grimsby Town, and Keith Alexander, now twenty-nine, was a full-time professional footballer. With a two-year contract to boot.

Another pleasing element of his move to the Mariners was his reunion with his best friend John Cockerill. There were strong similarities with their transfers to the club. John had given up his job as a lorry driver to play full-time and Keith left Contano Aluminium in Spalding where he'd worked as a draughtsman. Both were late going into League football, even later in Keith's case, unbeknown to his manager, and both were effectively taking a pay cut to do so. Their basic wage at Grimsby Town would be less than the money they received working and playing part-time. Neither of them cared because this was their chance to make a name for themselves.

Cockerill would often echo others when he described his friend's ability. He would say how good Keith was at keeping the ball and bringing others into play. He could confirm that he had self-control and played with a smile on his face. However, his description would also include one part of his pal's repertoire that many others often missed.

"Keith was different to a lot of players when it came to ball control," said Cockerill. "So many times the opposition, and his team-mates for that matter, thought he'd lost the ball. But he hadn't. He knew where it was and he'd still got it. From looking like the ball had gone loose, a long leg would stretch out and his foot would curl around it. The nearest defender would be out of the game and we were off towards their goal again."

Cockerill already lived in Grimsby with his parents. Keith mentioned he was looking for somewhere to stay in the area during the week and John readily invited him to stay in the family home. Keith enjoyed living there and John's mum soon liked looking after their polite, friendly lodger with his easy-going manner. Often Mrs Cockerill put the evening meal in front of each of the three men at her table, only for John and his dad to look down at their own modest portions, then look at Keith's generous helping and finally look at each other with mild dismay as Keith, oblivious, tucked into a huge plate of food. A few months later, John made the decision to use his football wages wisely and bought his own place in the town. Keith moved in with him and, although he lost out on this meal-time favouritism, the two mates continued to enjoy working and socialising together.

Keith relished his new full-time role. He loved the training and he watched and listened to Buckley to see how he did things. As usual, he wanted to improve as a player there and then, but he also wanted to learn as much as he could for the future, when maybe somewhere sometime he might be the man in charge. He made his debut for Grimsby in their first home game of the season against Torquay. He wore the number eleven shirt and played well as they scraped home 1-0.

Unfortunately, the number of new players being used meant that the team took a long time to gel and by the end of October the Mariners were languishing near the bottom of the table. The board and the fans, well used to failure, began to worry once more. As can often happen, and as wished for by many a manager, the FA Cup came along to distract the struggling players from their weekly travails, and things suddenly started to get interesting.

Keith and his team-mates couldn't have had a harder start to their cup campaign. Sleeping giants Wolves were on the road to recovery and sat at the top of Division Three. This was in the days when the divisions were numbered simply, and properly some would say, from one at the top to four at the bottom. Competing against the highest placed club in the first round draw at their place meant, therefore, that Grimsby Town were given little chance. It suited them and they played out of their skins.

Whether John Cockerill's corner was meant for his best pal's head the Mariners' fans would never know, but it curled right into the top corner of the Wolves net, so they didn't care either. Grimsby hung on for a superb 1-0 win and suddenly the players started to have some self-belief. Next up were Rotherham United, who were top of Division Four and who were beaten 3-2 in a thrilling game at Blundell Park. Just like every lower league player who makes it to round three of the FA Cup, Keith listened to the draw hoping his team were paired against any one of the biggest clubs in Division One. He wasn't disappointed when they got Middlesbrough away. On a crisp January afternoon, he ran out at Ayresome Park to face a home team that, only a few days earlier, had beaten Manchester United in a league game on that very pitch.

Again they played like heroes, chasing every ball, closing down the home team's attacks and creating a few chances for themselves. Grimsby won 2-1 and the huge away following saluted their team at the end. Such cup triumphs were bound to lift the players' confidence when it came to their league programme. Results did indeed improve and the Mariners slowly but surely climbed away from the bottom of Division Four. In the fourth round, they drew Reading, from a division higher, at home.

When the game ended 1-1, most people thought Grimsby's chance of progress had gone and the cup journey was about to end. Prompted by Buckley's insistence on his team keeping possession, his players nullified the home team's attacks in the replay and they came away with another 2-1 victory.

By now, Grimsby Town had a lot to thank the FA Cup for. They'd gone much further than anyone had expected, the fans were now beyond excited and were electrified by it, and it had rubbed off on their league form. It had turned their season around. It was also responsible for the arrival of another significant newcomer to the club. The person who thought that a large inflatable fish was an appropriate accessory for Mariners fans to wave around whenever their team ran out on to the pitch or scored a goal could have risked being collected by earnest looking men in hospital issue coats to be taken away for analysis. Not so. Harry the Haddock became the well-known trade-mark for Grimsby's cup exploits and he was soon as famous as the players who were doing the business.

Early on in the fifth round tie away at First Division Wimbledon, John Cockerill swung in a corner and Keith's header hit the back of the net before anyone could move. Keith wheeled away towards the 7,000 Grimsby fans who outnumbered the home supporters in a crowd of over 12,000. Nearly every one of those away fans waved a Harry the

Haddock in celebration and the sight was both exhilarating and surreal. Many wise old football fans from clubs at all levels who thought they'd seen everything in the game must have been open-mouthed when Keith Alexander's celebrations in front of a backcloth of thousands of large fish featured so dramatically in the cup highlights programme on TV that weekend.

Sadly the home team got on top and triumphed 3-1 so the cup run was over, but no-one connected with Grimsby could have been disappointed. It had lifted them all, they'd enjoyed the thrills and spills of it and the team had gained the confidence to finish the season well, climbing up to ninth spot. Years later, Keith was asked about Harry the Haddock. He said he'd been given one and he'd put it in the loft as a souvenir. Asked if he'd still got it, he said he hadn't seen it for a while. He added that he thought it had maybe gradually deflated, which was probably why it was no longer visible, but he was sure it was still in there somewhere.

By now, Keith and his wife Val had split up. During the close season he regularly met her in Sleaford, between Grimsby and Boston, to collect their two sons, Matthew and Paul, so that he could spend time with them. More often than not, he'd head for Nottingham so he could take them to see the family and they could do things in the city centre.

"Dad would take us to lunch somewhere or to buy us things and all the time people would shout 'Hello big man!' and 'How's it going Keith!' across the street to him," said Matt. "Everyone seemed to know him and they all wanted to chat to him. I soon learned how he knew how to find things out about people so he could have a good chat and a joke with them. He never just got conversations over with."

Keith was looking forward to the new season. Buckley had proved himself as a manager and he wasn't about to change the way he wanted his team to play. It would be good passing football or nothing. The team was strengthened by the acquisition of strikers Tony Rees and Gary Birtles, who'd won a European Cup winners medal with Nottingham Forest.

"I might have played at a high level with Forest, Manchester United and England," said Birtles "And my career might have been drawing to a close. But I was like any player – it's an anxious moment going into a new dressing room and meeting your new team-mates. At Grimsby the first guy to come up to me to greet me was Keith Alexander. Then he introduced me to everyone else. We were both Nottingham lads and we got on from the first minute we met."

Grimsby got off to a good start, losing only one of their first six games. By now, Keith had met Helen, his new partner. In the second year of a two-year contract, Keith was still cagey about his actual age because he didn't want to alert his manager so, for quite a while, even Helen thought he was a little bit younger than he actually was. Even the *Rothmans Yearbook*, the bible of football facts and figures, had got his date of birth down as 14th November, 1958.

In October, Grimsby took on local rivals Lincoln City at Sincil Bank. Town had started to struggle a bit and, if they wanted to mount a serious promotion challenge, the last thing they needed was to lose to their near neighbours. Grimsby dominated but came away with a 1-1 draw, with Keith getting their goal. It wasn't all he did, when the issue of racism cropped up again. As his team prepared for a corner, a home fan threw a banana at him. I remember seeing him pick it up and hand it to the referee, his arms then outstretching and his shoulders shrugged representing a sort of 'How can this happen ?' gesture. Sadly, the referee just shrugged back. There was no reaction from the crowd in that part of the ground either, such as identifying the offender to a steward. It just wasn't done because that sort of incident still wasn't considered a big deal in those days.

After the Christmas period, the Mariners were in fifteenth place and everyone at the club thought promotion was by now impossible. Keith had got only one goal, that one at Lincoln, until he scored in three successive matches, and the

New Year saw his team embark on a remarkable run. Tony Rees, Gary Birtles and Keith scored regularly, the passing game clicked and Grimsby lost only four out of twenty-five games in spring 1990. In March, they won seven out of seven, conceding only two goals and climbed to second in the table. With four games to go, Grimsby knew that if they were to win at Southend then promotion would be secured.

Keith was already a cult hero among the fans for both his carefree attitude and his ball skills. They all loved his habit of looking like he hadn't a clue where the ball was when, in fact, he had it totally under control. In the vital game at Roots Hall, it looked to everyone like he'd taken this illusion one step further. A cross came over, Keith tried to volley the ball goalwards and completely missed it. It hit the knee of his standing leg and went in, totally bamboozling the home keeper. While Keith was looking around wondering where the ball was, his team-mates and the Town fans massed behind the goal went mad. Then, realising what had happened, he wheeled away to celebrate, the last in the ground to know he'd scored. He notched a second goal in more conventional fashion, Grimsby won 2-0 and promotion was assured.

Gary Birtles scored a hat-trick in the Mariners' last home game, in front of a huge crowd. Keith had made thirty-eight appearances that season and netted a dozen goals. Tony Rees pipped him to the leading scorer accolade by one goal. Amazingly, Keith had made sixteen of his appearances from the subs bench, so his goal-scoring record was all the more impressive. He'd made a significant contribution to Grimsby's success and he'd achieved his first honour as a full-time professional. It felt good at the time and, in the longer term, he had acquired even more experience for when, or if, he was to become a coach or a manager.

Another achievement came Keith's way in 1990 when he was chosen to represent St Lucia. He played three times in all, including an appearance in the Vieux Fort national stadium. St Lucia were, as an international team, in their infancy when it came to their aspirations on the national stage and they didn't attempt to qualify for the World Cup through CONCACAF until the mid-90s. However, they competed in the Gold Cup and Caribbean Cup, and Keith was proud to wear the colours of his parents' home island.

Back in north Lincolnshire he pondered if it was time to move on. He knew he would be offered a contract for another year at Blundell Park but the club had moved up a level and he'd been on the bench plenty of times already. It was likely he'd be a substitute more often than gaining a place in the starting eleven. If Buckley signed another striker or two, he might not even get that. One night that summer he was slumped comfortably on the settee at John Cockerill's house when the phone rang in the hallway. John answered it and struggled to understand the almost incoherent pidgin-English being spoken to him by the caller. He held his hand over the mouthpiece and shouted through to Keith.

"It's some foreign manager. Wants to speak to you. Wants you to sign for him," said John. In the late '80s and early '90s, managers of Football League clubs were almost exclusively ex-players from the home nations. Foreign managers were managers of foreign clubs. Keith was therefore more than sceptical about the call and was convinced it was a prank by one of their team-mates. He issued an expletive-laden reply and turned up the volume on the television. John urged him to come through and take the call which, with a resigned sigh, Keith did. And so it was that he was to agree terms with Danny Bergara, the Uruguayan manager of Stockport County of Division Four.

*****

Bergara might have struggled in his efforts to learn English but he'd done a good job at Edgeley Park. He'd guided County away from the relegation zone in spring 1989, and they'd made it to the play-offs the following season. He was another manager who saw that Keith Alexander could be the piece in the jigsaw that meant his side went one step further this time round. The season got underway and, as the manager expected, his side were soon near the top of the table. They stayed there, too, and were to go on to win the promotion their previous season's form suggested they might. It wasn't working out for Keith too well, though, and he managed only nine appearances and two as substitute between September and early December.

Over in deepest Lincolnshire, things weren't going very well at Lincoln City either. Chairman John Reames admitted that manager Allan Clarke, the ex-Leeds and England striker, had 'lost the dressing room', and he was sent on his way. In November, with the Imps near the foot of the league and the fans fearing another relegation and more non-league misery, he appointed club captain Steve Thompson to replace him. Thompson was in his second spell as a centre-half at Sincil Bank and was a favourite with the supporters with his no-nonsense manner. He was honest and straight-talking, too, which was another likeable side to him. He demonstrated this on his first day in charge by saying he'd get the sack eventually because every manager does, especially at Lincoln, but he'd do his best to turn the club around in the meantime. Thompson said he would abandon Clarke's insistence on playing an intricate passing game because it didn't work. He said his players would play whatever way they had to in order to get enough points to stay up, but he convinced Reames that a couple of new faces were needed to help make this happen.

"I knew Keith when he lived in Boston with Val," said Thompson. "And he and his mate Jim Kabia played for the Ferryboat pub, my local, when Keith was at Barnet. Even though he shouldn't have done, of course. And I played against him when Lincoln played Grimsby in the last couple of seasons."

Keith joined Lincoln from Stockport for a fee of £7,500. Thompson told a local reporter that he could have got a Skoda for that and the Skoda would have been quicker, but this was probably more of a measure of the new manager's humour than a reflection of Keith's pace, even if he was nearing veteran stage. Thompson also persuaded the board to splash out £55,000 on another striker, Jason Lee from Charlton.

"I had no experience or guile in the team," explained Thompson. "I'd got a lot of young players and I knew Keith and Jason would bring some maturity and strength to the team. Set them an example – that sort of thing."

The two new forwards couldn't have been more different. Keith was, by now, almost famous for being relaxed and showing self-control on the football pitch. Lee, on the other hand, was a human battering ram. People suspected him of polishing his elbows as well as his boots before a match, such was the punishment opposing centre-halves would suffer. The new strike partnership was therefore a mixture of smiling subtlety one minute and grievous bodily harm the next. Reames and his board couldn't care less, though, because although Keith and Jason Lee didn't score that many goals, young fellow striker Tony Lormor fed off them and bagged a good few. Long-serving centre-half Grant Brown steadied the defence, too, and the team registered three wins and three draws in January and climbed away from the drop zone.

"We used to say that Keith should be banned from the team bus for bringing bad luck," joked Thompson. "He went to Torquay three times with Stockport. The first two were postponed through frost late on. Then we went and it was called off after we'd got all the way there. That meant he went to Torquay five times in one season. That must be a record."

Lincoln lost only three out of their last seventeen games and finished halfway in Division Four. They beat Carlisle 6-2 in the last game of the season at Sincil Bank and, after the worry of relegation, there were smiles all round.

Keith agreed to extend his contract with the Imps but he knew his playing days were numbered. He was also tired of moving from club to club and living in different places, sometimes out of a suitcase. He'd always found it easy to get on with people and make friends but he felt at home at Lincoln and got on especially well with people at the club and in the city. Grant Brown had been at Sincil Bank since 1986 and he had only good words for his team-mate.

"As a player he was gangly, awkward and smiled to himself a lot. He'd never clatter anyone and we often wished he would," said Brown. "But he was a lovely guy. He had his sayings like 'You've always got a chance with a striker like me in the team.' And he used to carry a photo of himself around that he'd get out and make us laugh. It was from when he was at Barnet. He was sitting in a bright orange Ford Capri looking out the window grinning and he'd got a huge afro haircut. Priceless."

Keith and Helen moved into a flat on Bailgate in the historic centre of Lincoln. As Keith threw himself into pre-season training, Thompson had talks with his chairman about changes at the club. He told Reames that he'd operated last season with only a physio alongside him. He needed help. As well as that, the club hadn't got a reserve side or a youth squad. Eventually Reames was persuaded.

"A club needs kids to bring in some vibrancy," explained the manager. "Of course you need them as a way of producing players and you might just unearth a gem. But they lift a club. If you've got some cheeky little fuckers around all the time it keeps the pro's on their toes." There was only one candidate for the new youth team coach position.

"Keith's still needed as a player to guide the younger first teamers, but he's a good influence on everyone, not just established players," said Thompson. "And he's someone I can trust. He's doing his badges and he knows how to win people over. He'll be ideal."

Things had come together perfectly for Keith. He still wanted to play, but the club had some good young strikers in the squad like Tony Lormor and Peter Costello. It was likely that Jason Lee would be first choice to lead the attack, too.

Most of all, though, Keith had always had a burning ambition to coach players and manage a team. So when Thompson rang him one evening to offer him the youth team job he accepted straight away. It was the natural next step in his career in football.

Keith was in and out the first team as the season got underway. Results were mixed, but the Imps fans suffered in silence one evening in September when Barnet, newly promoted from the Conference after several near misses, once because of Lincoln, came to Sincil Bank and won 6-0. Revenge indeed. Keith would be asked to warm up the players during training and to do some coaching. He had one-to-one sessions with some of the players and worked with Jason Lee a lot to add more than just aggression to his repertoire.

Keith and his boss sought out good quality youngsters for the new youth squad from a number of sources. They also set up a series of open trials. A boy from Nottingham turned up to one and scored goals from all angles, so Keith was quick to thrust a pen in his hand. It wasn't always easy to see potential talent when each young man nervously tried to impress, sometimes too hard, but in this case a confident Darren Huckerby, who went on to play at the highest level, stood out a mile. It was difficult to assess which lads might eventually make it as first team players in such a short time and Keith would consider anything about them that might give him a clue.

A composed youngster playing in defence looked the part, except he was fairly small for his age. Thompson said that the size of his dad might give them a clue if the player would grow enough. Keith asked him if his mum and dad were watching and he pointed across to them. They remarked that his dad was small too, only about 5'6". The player quietly corrected them and confirmed that the guy was his step-dad and his actual father was 6'5". Keith quickly made sure young Matt Carbon, a future Imps star, joined the others who had already been signed up.

In the first fifteen games of the season the Imps managed to score only eight goals. Then, in consecutive derbies at home to Scunthorpe and away to Doncaster, they scored nine. Lormor got four as they won the games 4-2 and 5-1. Near the bottom of the table in January, Lincoln lost only once in their last seventeen games, winning the last seven. In April, Keith's hard work with the youngsters started to bear fruit when eighteen-year-old Ben Dixon was chosen as substitute for the home game against Maidstone United. If he was nervous when he was told he was making the step up, he soon relaxed when he saw that Keith, his boss, was on the bench with him.

Thompson's team had done well, finishing tenth. He had made the club some money, too, selling Matt Dickins to Blackburn Rovers and Shane Nicholson to Derby. The board reported that the club had made a profit – the first time they'd done so for years. Keith and Helen were pleased that things were going well with the youth set-up and the club in general, so they bought a house in Dunholme, a village to the north of the city.

Without winning a game, Lincoln City became a Division Three club in the summer of 1992. Just before the start of the season, the Premiership was formed, so the divisions below this modestly titled body were numerically revised. Whatever the division was titled, the Imps were joint favourites to finish top of it after their cracking end to the previous campaign. In August, the youth team started their season with a 4-0 win over Port Vale. Keith had been delighted with the progress Darren Huckerby had been making and his hat-trick in that game encouraged him even more. He knew that, with a bit more careful nurturing, the lad would go on to serve the first team well and, such was his potential, hopefully the scouts from much bigger clubs would start congregating. This would be good for the player and his career and good for the club and its bank balance.

Keith was still in the first team squad but only made the bench ten times during the season and was never in the starting eleven. He wasn't put out by this one bit, because his job now was to develop other talents after years of putting his own to the test. Thompson showed faith in his youth team coach's skills by giving Matt Carbon his debut in the team but, as the season neared its end, Lincoln had never really looked like threatening the automatic promotion places. Despite this, it wasn't results that were causing problems for the manager. The board weren't too concerned about the club failing to make it to Division Two.

The squad was pretty good and they were delighted too that Keith was developing some exciting young prospects. The youth squad had finished fourth in the Midland Purity League and they'd been up against sides from clubs much higher in the Football League pyramid. Keith had encouraged them to play attractive football and they had an unbeaten run of five wins and two draws as the season drew to a close. Ben Dixon and Matt Carbon had been called up to play for an FA Youth XI in a match against an FA Schools XI. However, when it came to first team affairs some of the directors were becoming disenchanted with Thompson's manner and they felt he didn't show them enough respect.

City's last match was a home game against Darlington. The Imps weren't mathematically out of the running for a play-off place, but it would take a cricket score against their north-east opponents and defeats for their rivals elsewhere for it to happen. Keith was looking forward to the close season. Not for a rest, but to start seeking out new recruits for his youth section and to push for one or two of the older ones to be granted full-time professional contracts. On the Thursday night, chairman John Reames rang him up. Keith's career was about to change direction once again.

5

Taking Over the Team, Learning Lessons

"There is not the remotest possibility of Keith Alexander going anywhere at this stage"
John Reames

Steve Thompson was not a happy man. In fact, he was livid and wanted answers. He'd taken Lincoln City to the edge of the play-offs and they'd been making money. He just couldn't understand why he'd been given the sack three days before the final game of the season. When chairman John Reames asked Keith to be caretaker-manager for the Darlington match, he readily accepted. It would be the first managerial role of his career, even if it was for only one game. Keith was surprised Thompson had gone, but there would be no point in telling Reames he was wrong. In football, 'the king is dead, long live the king'.

Keith instantly showed faith in the young players who had developed so well under him that season. He picked Matt Carbon to play in defence and gave seventeen-year-old Ben Dixon his first-team debut. Another youngster, Steve Parkinson, was on the bench. Lincoln played well and deservedly beat Darlington 2-0. Dixon, especially, had performed well, setting up the opening goal. Even though the Imps missed out on a play-off place by a point, with Bury pipping them for the last spot, the fans went home happy. After the match, Keith didn't mince words when it came to declaring his interest in getting the manager's job on a permanent basis.

"I've got the job for now, so it's up to the others to take it off me," he was reported as saying. Less than two weeks after the end of the season his wish came true and he was appointed. To say he'd got the job permanently would, strictly speaking, be a little bit optimistic because he became the club's eighth gaffer in fifteen years, but he'd already made history. He became the first black manager in the Football League. Ed Stein had done it, having been in temporary charge at Barnet, but Keith was the first to be given a full contract.

"I'm thrilled," said Keith at a press conference. "I'm honoured to get the manager's job at a progressive club like Lincoln City."

His first move in the hot seat was to try and get John Cockerill on board as his assistant but, keen as he was, John couldn't extricate himself from his contract at Grimsby. Keith had been John's best man at his wedding earlier in the year but friendship wasn't the only motive for bringing him in. He felt he would be an ideal number two. It wasn't to be and, undeterred, Keith set about looking for new players and arranging friendly matches for the build-up to the new season. Centre-half Mick Smith was signed from Notts County, along with winger Steve Mardenborough from Darlington. Using his knowledge of the non-league scene, Keith set up friendly games with several local sides. At the end of July, they played away at Frickley Athletic and he commented that he knew it would be a good test.

"This will be a big game for Frickley," he observed. "I know when I played non-league football we always looked forward to playing Football League sides."

Next up was a home game against Barnet whose eventful history under the departed Fry and Flashman was no less colourful now. Gaining promotion had nearly cost them their very existence so they approached the new season with hardly any players and having to prove to the Football League that they would be able to fulfil their fixtures. Keith was pleased to help his old club and when his team beat their collection of youngsters and trialists 3-1 it had given his players a good run-out in front of the Lincoln faithful. Every club tries for at least one 'prestige' friendly before the action proper starts. It gives the players a good test and the chairman hopes it brings in a decent chunk of gate money. Lincoln hosted Nottingham Forest in their main pre-season game and it certainly worked in terms of a good attendance and healthy gate receipts. It proved to be a real challenge for the Imps players though, with Forest winning easily and Stan Collymore scoring a hat-trick in their 5-1 victory.

Three days before the first league match of the season, Keith spoke to a local reporter about his side, their prospects and his exciting attacking options. He'd agreed to let Jason Lee sign for Southend, where Fry had arrived as manager, but he still had six players vying for four striking or attacking midfield places. One of them, the popular Tony Lormor, had suffered a bad knee injury but was on the mend.

"Tony is making good progress and he's training and playing games," explained Keith. "When it comes to getting back in the side, he's there or thereabouts. It's great to have him back fighting for his place again."

The season started and, despite not registering a win in their first four games, Keith and his team celebrated victory, strange as that may seem. They lost narrowly in the heat at Colchester and a week later drew at home to Darlington. Either side of that first league game at Sincil Bank they played a two-legged League Cup tie against Port Vale from a division higher. At Vale Park, Tony Lormor scored twice as Lincoln came back from 2-0 down to draw 2-2. A week later in the second leg, two hours of football remained scoreless and the Imps went through on the away goals rule. The victory was made all the more significant when Lincoln drew Everton in the next round. A good week was rounded off when Keith enjoyed his first win as a Football League manager. His team won at Hereford with another new signing, David 'Magic'

Johnson, scoring on his debut.

One policy Keith adopted was to speak to the chairman and directors after every game. Win, lose, or draw, he thought it was only right to join them in the boardroom. His predecessor hadn't been so forthcoming, often leaving the ground straight after a defeat. But Keith didn't do it because Thompson hadn't or because he wanted to suck up to the top brass. They employed him and they deserved to speak to him. He might not fancy it sometimes and they might ask odd questions, but Keith wanted to involve them, like he wanted to involve the staff and the fans in what he was trying to do.

Next up were Chester at home but a good midweek crowd of over 4,000 saw the Imps get soundly beaten 3-0. Keith was never shy at talking to the local media. He felt it was his duty to keep the fans informed.

"The buck stops with me and I'll have to do something about it," he told the *Lincolnshire Echo*. "The fans are being lenient with us because we are trying to play football."

After another two defeats in which the side again failed to score, chief executive Geoff Davey sounded less understanding.

"The chairman and directors are entirely dissatisfied with things at present and changes may well be on the cards," he said in a surprisingly blunt interview, bearing in mind the manager had only been in charge for six league games. "I must confirm, however, Keith's position is not in doubt," he added, no doubt bringing some relief to supporters thinking yet another change at the top was imminent. Keith responded by putting virtually all the first team squad on the transfer list. Long-serving Grant Brown, regular midfielder John Schofield and star striker Tony Lormor weren't exempt from this drastic move. Only the handful of new signings and the younger players survived.

"We are playing good football but we need results," said Keith, adding "This is not an idle threat."

The cup-tie brought them all some welcome relief. Over

9,000 fans filled Sincil Bank to see the Imps take on Everton, who were currently fourth in the Premiership behind Manchester United, Arsenal, and Aston Villa. In a thrilling game, Lincoln eventually lost 4-3 with Paul Rideout getting a hat-trick for the visitors, including the winner five minutes from time. This time Keith was full of praise for all his players and the occasion seemed to lift them as they resumed their league programme. A 4-3 win over Northampton was followed by two wins and a draw in the next three games. In true boardroom fashion, Davey was suddenly enthusing about things, especially when it came to some unexpected income.

"Playing Everton home and away could bring us in about £50,000," he explained. "That's a fair chunk in a turnover of two million." City lost the second leg 4-2 at Goodison Park, where Tony Cottee scored two late goals to finish off Lincoln's challenge, but again Keith was complimentary about his players' attitude and performance.

The run of form in the league came to an end with defeat at Chesterfield and this set a pattern leading up to Christmas. The team would get a few decent results and optimism would rise and then they'd slip up. Two wins and a draw in November were followed by a pasting against Walsall where they let in three in thirteen minutes and went on to lose 5-2. Although Lincoln were tenth in the division, once more the chief executive didn't mince his words.

"Our form last season suggested we could be a top seven club," he told the local paper. "What we need is a sequence of wins to get up there, not just these little unbeaten runs." No pressure then.

If the men in suits were becoming irritated by some of the league performances, the cup competitions were taking their minds off Lincoln's inconsistency. Winning at Witton in the first round of the FA Cup was rewarded with a home tie against First Division Bolton Wanderers. Sky Sports decided this potential David versus Goliath fixture was something their viewers would like to see and chairman Reames was pleased they did.

"This is another boost to our finances. We'll also be on the BBC highlights programme so that will help too," he said. "We should attract some good national advertising so we're very pleased."

His chief executive revealed even more good news.

"We'll probably net £80,000 from the cup game," Davey explained. "And Keith Scott, who we sold to Wycombe, has just signed for Swindon in the Premiership. The sell-on clause will be worth nearly £70,000 to us. We might be able to help Keith strengthen his squad with some of that."

Led by striker Owen Coyle, recently signed from Airdrie for £250,000, Bolton pushed the Imps aside at Sincil Bank. Over 8,000 people watched as goals from Alan Thompson, Phil Brown and Coyle put the visitors 3-0 up before 'Magic' Johnson scored a late consolation. Keith was far from happy with his side's display and they got both barrels at full time. Grant Brown reflected on Keith's managerial style compared to his previous gaffer.

"They are totally different characters," he explained. "Keith is relaxed and laid back, but he also has his own way of being hard on us. He doesn't shout and bawl but he's made us come in a lot more on Sundays if we've played badly the day before than we ever did under Steve. I'm enjoying playing for Keith, though. I had a chance to move to Preston but I decided to stay because I like it here."

Keith may have had moments when it came to putting his foot down, but the players liked him and the way he did things. Young Matt Carbon was impressing everyone with his progress in training and in youth and reserve team games. Off the pitch, things weren't going so well for him and his homesickness was getting worse. Knowing Keith as she did, Helen wasn't at all surprised when the bashful young defender turned up on their doorstep with a couple of suitcases. Keith's solution to the problem was to tell the lad he would be lodging with them for a few months. Matt soon settled in and became much happier.

The fans liked Keith too. He was good with the media and the messages he got across, but he also made the effort to engage with supporters individually. Karl Mercer was one such Imps fan who enjoyed meeting the manager.

"I was lucky enough to be involved in Football Challenge 93, a charity event which involved visiting all 92 League clubs to collect a piece of memorabilia to auction off in aid of the Imperial Cancer Research Fund," he explained. "Needless to say, when we turned up at Lincoln, I was very excited at the prospect of meeting someone from my own club. I was very pleasantly surprised when, in fact, it was Keith who came out to present us with a signed Lincoln City football. We had our photo taken with the big man on the pitch. To the left of us in front of the South Park Stand, the youth team were training, including Darren Huckerby.

"I was standing there on the hallowed turf with a football in my hand with a massive urge to run towards the other goal and smash it into the back of the net. Big Keith detected the glint in my eye, winked at me and said 'go on then, go for it'. I chucked the ball on to the grass and dribbled expertly to the edge of the penalty area cheered on by my colleagues, Keith and the whole youth team. The pressure was building up inside me and, in my haste, I hit the ball with my left foot; very much my weaker foot. I missed the open goal by a mile! I could hear Keith's laughter and he shouted across to the youth team 'Don't worry, I'll not be offering him a contract lads' and they all laughed and cheered."

In December, Lincoln City made another appearance on television. To be more precise, manager Keith Alexander did. The people at Sky had been very impressed with what they found at Sincil Bank when they covered the Bolton game. They liked Keith's attempts at getting his team to play entertaining football and they admired the work he was doing with the younger players. Consequently, Andy Gray and a film crew turned up to record two episodes of 'The Boot Room', a documentary that looked behind the scenes at a football club and investigated a manager's methods. The fact that the programme usually only featured Premiership clubs and managers was a measure of how much the erstwhile presenter and his colleagues had been taken by the Imps boss.

After a couple of good results that month, the Lincoln faithful looked forward to the derby match with Scunthorpe at Sincil Bank two days after Christmas with renewed optimism. Keith made sure the players were fit and ready by getting them in for training on Boxing Day morning. This meant that those who lived away had to curtail their family celebrations. Grant Brown, for one, had to set off from his parents' home in Sunderland at six o'clock in the morning after a restrained Christmas Day, but he was used to Keith's discipline and appreciated what his gaffer wanted from him and his team-mates. A boisterous crowd of over 6,000 saw the Imps triumph 2-0. As the New Year approached, Lincoln had enjoyed some exciting Cup games, the finances were looking good and they were handily placed just outside the play-off places. With the money there to strengthen the squad, everyone, including the manager, the board and the fans, thought the team would push on and climb the table.

*****

Then it all went wrong. Home defeats against Scarborough and Wycombe were followed by defeat at Doncaster where new boss Ian Atkins had brought in former Imps manager Steve Thompson as his assistant. Keith had already made it clear to his chairman that he wanted to sign new players and the defeats made this all the more urgent.

"The chairman, directors and manager are all in agreement that we need to infuse some new players into the squad," confirmed Geoff Davey. Then, diplomatic as ever, and no doubt irritating his manager by criticising a player's performances, he described the situation with defender David Hurst who was currently with the club on loan. "We might extend his loan by another month. He played well in his first two games but not so well in his next two."

Keith hadn't managed to infuse any new players into the team that drew at Chester, and another two games brought only one point. Even the cup magic had gone when the Imps lost 2-1 after extra time at Carlisle in the Auotoglass Trophy northern semifinal in mid-February. But the manager was still optimistic, even if his comments were this time met with some scepticism by disillusioned supporters.

"Don't rule us out of the promotion picture," he said defiantly. "From now until the end of the season we're going to play open attacking football. We've had a good run in all the cups but the league and promotion is what's important to us and, despite our lowly position, we are going for it."

Strong words indeed, but they seemed even more hollow to Lincoln supporters as the final whistle blew at the end of the next home match. The Imps had lost 1-0 to Wigan, it was their sixth home defeat of the season, they were now fifth from bottom, and they still hadn't won in 1994. The attendance was poor, just over 2,500, but those who were there let the chairman know they weren't happy. Chants of 'sack the board' and 'Davey out' were heard as the players trooped off.

"Chants against the board aren't going to change anything," responded the under-fire chairman. "We need supporters to get behind us. There is no question about the future of Keith Alexander. He wants us to play good football and we want him to build a side to do that. There is not the remotest possibility of Keith going anywhere at this stage."

"Things are not going well but I don't feel under any pressure," Keith told the local media. "People are saying our season is over but our aim is to get out of the division and I don't think we are out of things just yet. And I'm not looking over my shoulder either."

The following week that infusion of new players finally

took place. Tony Daws arrived from Grimsby Town and Alan Johnson was signed from Wigan Athletic for a sizeable transfer fee. Keith's new men brought him some relief from the doom and gloom by playing well and contributing to a 3-1 win against Hereford. Another loss followed at Preston but this was not unexpected, with a lot of clubs that season coming away from Deepdale unhappy about their new plastic pitch and the advantage they felt that it gave the home side. The travelling Imps fans then enjoyed a win at Shrewsbury. A rare three points was reward enough for the journey on a cold Tuesday evening but they'd also had the privilege of witnessing Darren Huckerby's debut.

He came on as a substitute and scored the winner after a jinking run through the home defence and that one bit of action was enough to convince everyone that the slim young lad in a red-and-white striped shirt was a star in the making. Before the game, supporter Karl Mercer left the confines of the away end to be one of a party of fundraisers who were presenting a cheque to a representative of the Imperial Cancer Research Fund. They had completed their trek to all the football grounds of England and Wales and had collected their sponsors' donations.

"Keith came over to me and said 'hello again' and asked for my programme," said Karl. "He said he would take it into the dressing room and get all the players to sign it for me. It showed me what a true gent he was. The fact he even remembered me was enough."

Such pleasant vibes soon evaporated, though. A combination of further defeats and foul weather meant that only 1,600 fans turned up at Sincil Bank for a midweek fixture against Colchester. It was the lowest home gate since the return to the Football League. Although Lincoln were down among the strugglers in the division, Keith insisted on telling the local media that his side could still be up with the 'leading lights'. Maybe, by now, even some of the most loyal fans were becoming a little weary of his bravado.

In the lead-up to transfer deadline day, the board put their money where their mouths were by giving their manager the funds to sign two more players. Defender Nicky Platnauer joined the club, followed by keeper Andy Leaning who was given a two-and-a-half year contract. They weren't the only new faces at the club though, and the appearance of another one was quite unexpected. Standing alongside Keith in the dug-out as the team kicked off against Crewe Alexandra was Sam Ellis, a former Imps legend. Ellis was captain of Graham Taylor's record-breaking Lincoln City team of the 70s and had more recently been in charge at Bury and assistant manager at Manchester City. Keith had operated on his own all season and it was never made clear who instigated the arrival of someone alongside him at this stage of the campaign.

It might never have been explained but many suspected it was a change the board had brought about. Certainly the players didn't notice any animosity between the two men and maybe Keith didn't mind having someone to help with training and to bounce his ideas off. Whoever was behind the introduction of Ellis, they weren't prepared to admit it, and were even less likely to when the results didn't improve as the end of the season approached. In the space of two days in April over the Spring Bank Holiday, Lincoln lost at Scunthorpe and at home to Shrewsbury, their ninth defeat at Sincil Bank. They lay sixth from bottom, but surprisingly Keith was still telling the press he hadn't fully ruled out a play-off place. The fans weren't as generous and were saying they were tired of his team having lots of possession, passing the ball around too much without getting anywhere, and losing to sucker punches game after game.

A 2-2 draw at Scarborough, where the Imps surrendered a two-goal lead, was followed by a 0-0 bore-draw at home when the team was booed off at the full time whistle. Local radio reporter Andy Farrant was impressed by the way Keith dealt with the criticism.

"I got on very well with Keith. He was the nicest football

person I'd ever met," said Farrant. "He wouldn't tolerate fools and he always found time for an interview with me. As the season wore on, I never saw him weaken under pressure."

Down near the bottom but safe from relegation, Keith and his squad travelled to Torquay where they stayed overnight before their game at Plainmoor the next day. It was a pleasant evening and he gave in to the players' requests to be allowed to go for a walk before retiring to their rooms. "Have a beer, maybe two. But don't take the piss," he told them. He was quickly reminded that a manager can be fair to his players but he mustn't be a soft touch. The players did have two beers, but that was only in the first pub they called at. Then they had another one in the next pub down the road. And so on.

The next day, quite a few of them weren't quite as robust as they should have been. At the ground, as the players changed into their kit, goalkeeper Andy Leaning was taken ill and had to be replaced. Not long after kick-off, Torquay were 2-0 up. The team rallied and scored twice, only for the home side to get a late winner. Keith was far from happy with his players, especially the senior ones. The travelling directors weren't exactly ecstatic either when they found out about the playing squad's jolly excursion into town the night before.

The last home game of the season was soon upon them and, other problems aside, they hoped for a win to stir up a bit of optimism for the next campaign and for season ticket sales in the summer. At 1-1, Lincoln were well on top but against the run of play, visitors Walsall were the team to snatch the late winner. It was the Imps' nineteenth defeat of the season, they'd won only four games in 1994 and they were fifth from bottom. A draw at Gillingham in the final league game the following week kept them there. Keith finally admitted that things had not gone well when he spoke to the press after the final whistle.

"We haven't played well since Christmas," he admitted. "In fact our form has been a disaster. But in saying that, I like to think we are still going through a slight transitional stage.

The players I've brought in have shown the will to win. If I can bring in some more like them for next season we should do well."

The board and chief executive found themselves under fire too, and they weren't about to sit and take it. A lot of fans thought that redevelopment of the ground had taken priority over team affairs, with both ends having being rebuilt and a fine new 6,500 all-seater stand soon to replace the popular open terrace down one side. Geoff Davey angrily told the media that regulations prevented funding towards new parts of the stadium being diverted to the playing squad.

"Anyway," he added, "we have spent a great deal of money on players this season, more than any other club in our division. Disgruntled fans can't accuse us of putting the ground before the team."

Away from the difficulties at work, Keith was involved in a sideline that was proving both enjoyable and successful. So successful, in fact, that he would soon be making another playing appearance at Wembley. He'd kept in touch with friends at Ilkeston and had agreed to play now and again for Ilkeston Town Veterans. During the season, they'd entered the Umbro Veterans competition and the team, including Keith, his old friend Jim Kabia and other ex-pro's like Mansfield manager Andy King, had done pretty well. Keith played up front and was pleased to prove he hadn't lost his touch by scoring a few goals. In the semifinal against Blackburn Rovers he netted twice in a 2-1 win. The prize for the winners was appearing in the Umbro Veterans final to be played as part of the pre-match build-up before the next Charity Shield match between Manchester United and Blackburn Rovers at the national stadium. Keith was Wembley-bound once more.

Back at Sincil Bank he quickly set about announcing his retained list and breaking the grim news to players who wouldn't be kept on. Surprisingly, Grant Brown and John Schofield, both long-serving members of the squad and firm favourites with the fans, rejected their offers of new contracts.

Their manager was unmoved and confirmed that the terms put to them would not be improved. He also confirmed that his first priority over the summer would be to sign a tall target man to play alongside Tony Daws and an established central defender.

Resolving the contractual issues with Brown and Schofield, signing the two players he urgently needed, and all the other things a manager does during a close season sadly never happened. In the middle of April, Keith was sacked.

"The club has finished in its lowest league position in all but one of its last twenty years. It has been a disappointing season and Keith Alexander has been relieved of his duties," said a short statement from the club. Even now Keith was prepared to comment to the local media.

"If things aren't going well, you expect to lose your job in eighteen months or so," he said, his manner showing that his sacking was a genuine surprise to him. "I'm bitterly disappointed not to have been able to continue what I've started. People say we finished high up last season so I needn't have changed things round too much, but I wanted us to adopt a new style of play. I accept, though, that in the second half of the season things haven't gone particularly well."

It was clear that, despite a very poor second half to the campaign, Keith wasn't expecting to get the boot. It was also clear that Reames and his board still thought a lot of their ex-manager because they offered him a coaching job at the club, working with the youth squad again. Sensibly, Keith said he'd think it over. It wasn't in him to accept the role so quickly after they'd hurt him by taking away his managerial position. It would also be reckless to agree to do it when he didn't know who his new boss would be.

It proved to be a wise move. Two days later, the chairman proudly revealed that the Imps new manager would be none other than Sam Ellis. Suddenly, a lot of things became very clear. Keith didn't hold back.

"I have absolutely no doubt whatever that I will be a

successful manager at the top level," he barked. "I intend to learn from my stay at Sincil Bank. Sam was brought in when we had a bad spell. In fact, it was unfortunate our poor run of results coincided with Sam being here." With that he confirmed he wouldn't be taking the coaching job and his time at Lincoln City was over.

Losing his job wasn't Keith's only disappointment at this time, although it was by far the biggest one. The organisers of the Umbro Veterans tournament had been making some calls to the people who ran the Ilkeston Town team. They felt that their Blackburn Rovers counterparts had better players and more stars and would make more attractive finalists at Wembley, even though they'd lost the semifinal. They promised Ilkeston that they would indeed play at the great stadium but instead would represent England Veterans in a game preceding a future England international. So it transpired that Keith didn't enjoy that second Wembley experience after all. And to cap it all, Ilkeston never heard any more about that offer to represent England old-timers either.

*****

Keith had indeed learned a lot from his first spell in management. His season with Lincoln had confirmed that he knew what he was doing in a great many areas. The younger players were better footballers after a year under his wing and some were ready to prosper in the first team. He'd earned respect within the game and had remained popular at the club, even after all those defeats. So popular, in fact, that the hierarchy had changed their habits of a lifetime. Instead of banishing yet another unwanted manager to anywhere as long as it wasn't Sincil Bank, they'd wanted him to stay and develop the younger players still further. But that wasn't enough anymore. He'd experienced the buzz of being a manager and he wanted more. Except he'd also learned that next time some things would be done differently.

First off was how to play the game. Most managers want their team to play how they used to play. A big ugly ex-centre-half would have a team of giants muscling their way up the league. Long throws, set-pieces. Good football would come with confidence and confidence only came with winning. Footballers with flair would tell their team to pass and move, take the full-back on, get to the by-line. Keith had come from the second camp and, despite the assurances that he was doing the right thing, he'd ended up out of a job.

Playing football the right way had, to him, included bringing in youngsters and developing them for later. The board would be delighted then if a lad had first earned the team some results and then earned the club some money when he'd been snapped up. Except there often isn't time for that to happen if the fans lose patience and the board can't enjoy their post-match glass of wine because they're being shouted at as they disappear from the posh bit in the stand back into the boardroom.

When it came to the players, Keith already knew he'd need to get the balance right. A couple of defeats and harsh comments by a chief executive were no reason for a knee-jerk reaction that alienated his lads. He already knew that some players needed an arm round the shoulder and some needed a bollocking to get the best out of them. But they all needed to know who was boss. And in some ways, so did the chairman and his directors. It was part of the job when he listened to their questions after a game or at a board meeting, but he didn't have to take any of them saying how he should do the job, especially in the media.

When it came to the media, he realised his faith in his players and his bravado on their behalf probably didn't help. After a run of losses it wasn't wise to say the play-offs were still on, even if he thought it. Better that he played everything down. If you celebrate too much when things are going well, it hurts more when they aren't. Better that a few choice sayings are used to calm things down or put them in perspective.

So, for example, if in the future any team of his was up near the top, rather than waffle on about automatic promotion or winning the next few games, he'd just calmly say 'we'll be there or thereabouts' or something like that.

The main thing he'd picked up on in the 1993-94 season, though, was that the only thing that matters is results. Despite what anyone tells you. Get everyone at the club behind you, all in it together, and win. Don't expect players to do things they can't, just identify what they are good at and tell them to get on with it. Next time, if there was a next time, that's what he'd do. Get results.

6

Field Mill, Crossing the Irish Sea, Good Times at Ilkeston

"I fucking love your dad, I really do"
Paul Millership

Keith might have been unhappy at being sacked by Lincoln City, but his skills at coaching kids and his easy-going personality were by now well known. He and Helen were happy and settled in their house at Dunholme, just north of Lincoln, so he was pleased when Andy King, manager at nearby Mansfield Town, got in touch that summer.

Mansfield were owned by Keith Haslam, a very much hands-on individual as Stags fans were to find out years later. He had recruited King, the former Everton midfielder, who had previously worked as commercial executive at Luton and had not managed a club before. However, Haslam was impressed with his bubbly personality and felt he could galvanise Mansfield and their fans. They both felt that Keith would be the ideal foil for King. And so it was that Keith agreed to become assistant manager, tasked with helping with the first team, managing the reserves and overseeing the youth squad.

"I tried to go to a lot of games. Reserves and non-league, that sort of thing," said King. "Every time I sat down in the stand I saw Keith there. It seemed like I saw him at every single game. He'd been sacked at Lincoln and I thought that if he was prepared to work that hard, especially between jobs, then he'd do for me. I didn't really know him that well but as soon as he started at Field Mill I found out he was a nice guy and nice to work with. I also got to know pretty quickly how good with the players he was. I was the loud sort. I was brash and wanted to take on the world. Keith was a calming influence. I'd had Billy Dearden with me. He was the old-style quiet type. He'd left and Keith was the same sort of bloke. He was ideal."

Keith also retained his registration as a player and even made the bench as an unused substitute a couple of times as the Stags started the 1994-95 campaign in Division Three. The side was a mix of older established professionals like Steve Parkin and prolific striker Ian Wilkinson, along with some promising younger players like full-backs Ian Baraclough and Aidy Boothroyd. In an Auto Windscreens Trophy tie against Crewe Alexandra, Keith made his debut for the club, coming on after fifty-nine minutes. The side was depleted because of injury and suspensions but the introduction of the assistant manager into the action didn't weaken the team even further. Far from it because Keith quickly scored two goals to earn his side a 2-2 draw. At thirty-seven and, in fact, only six days away from his thirty-eighth birthday, he became Mansfield Town's oldest ever goal-scorer.

After a slow start, the first team under King and Keith hit form and from Christmas onwards it looked like automatic promotion was possible.

"Keith calmed the players down when they were wound up," said Boothroyd, recalling the management team's methods. "If any of us were angry we'd speak to him. He was approachable and we could trust him. He'd take our points to Andy in a way that we couldn't. He was a conduit between us and the manager. I was dropped once and I went off on one to him. He told me to calm down and said 'Just listen to yourself, that's no way to get back in. Get your head down, train hard and prove the gaffer wrong.' Andy kept his distance from the players – he needed to. Keith would relax with us and was one of the lads. But the big difference was that he wasn't just liked – he was respected. A manager or an assistant needs more than just being liked. Players need to respect a guy for it to work."

The finances were tight, though, so Keith's priority was to nurture young talent at the club and seek out new prospects elsewhere. Out of the blue, Andy King got a call from Northern Ireland manager Bryan Hamilton. He'd been asked by Cliftonville chairman Jim Boyce if he could use any of his contacts in England to find them an urgently needed striker. Hamilton and King used to be team-mates at Goodison Park and King suggested that his coach could help them out. He also thought that while he was there Keith might spot a few young prospects that he could bring back to Field Mill.

"I needed Keith with me," said King. "But there were advantages in him going over there for a short time. Anyway, no-one was on much money at Mansfield. I was happy for Keith to supplement his wages a bit."

Keith made his debut on 15th January in a league match at Portadown and a lot of fans still talk about the game as one of the best they've ever seen. Cliftonville led twice and were pegged back each time. Keith was running the show and made it 3-2 to the Reds after a mazy run, but once more the Ports drew level. Just when a draw looked likely, Keith threaded the ball through the home defence for Tim McCann to score the winner. Then Cliftonville played a midweek match against Linfield at Windsor Park in the quarter-final of the League Cup. He tore the opposing defence apart that night and, amazing the fans with his ball control, scored two goals that saw his team into the next round. He was invited to celebrate the win afterwards with members of the Red Army, one of whom was also celebrating the birth of another future Cliftonville supporter. Typically, Keith was delighted to spend the evening with them, although they noticed he was disciplined enough to stick to bottled beer rather than go on to the Bushmills whiskey like his new pals.

His next appearance was at the Oval, the home of Glentoran.

Unfortunately, his journey to Belfast had not been easy and his late arrival meant the game had already started and he had to sit on the bench. The Reds were 1-0 down so manager Marty Quinn brought Keith on and, within minutes of his arrival into the action, Cliftonville were 3-1 up. Keith had scored one and been instrumental in setting up two more for Gerry Flynn. Some Red Army guys saw and heard a couple of home fans giving Keith some pretty awful racial abuse. Keith could hear them but merely waved across smiling and blew kisses at them each time his team scored. A home fan then berated his offending colleagues, telling them that the more they'd abused Keith the better he'd played. In another game, this time at Solitude, the club's home ground, Keith brought a boring affair to life by setting off on a run down the right wing and whipping in a superb cross from the by-line that was headed in to give his side all three points.

Reds fans were dismayed when their new hero had to return home to England after only nine games. A Cliftonville fanzine, having already nicknamed Keith 'Hightower' after the Police Academy character, wrote about the impact he'd made and how they all loved him. Concluding an account of his time there it said: 'He came. He saw. He conquered. Alexander the Great!'

Mansfield's first team performed brilliantly in the second half of the season but two wins and seven draws in the last eleven games weren't enough to gain them a top three spot. In the play-offs they suffered a 6-3 aggregate defeat against near neighbours and bitter rivals Chesterfield so the campaign came to a disappointing end. Paul Holland had been a star all season and a mixture of good coaching and the experience he gained by being an integral part of a winning team meant he was rewarded by the national side. He was called up for England Under-21s and travelled to France with them to take part in the Toulon Tournament that summer. On his return he was sold to Sheffield United – a move he deserved after serving the Stags so well.

Keith continued to work for Mansfield the following season and, although the first team struggled like many sides do after a failed play-off attempt, he was pleased there was a good supply of youngsters pushing for a place in the first team. In November, the progress of one young player was very significant as far as Keith was concerned, for very different reasons. The Stags took on Lincoln City at Field Mill and sitting in the executive area he could see Kevin Keegan, Terry McDermott and Arthur Cox, the management team at Newcastle United. Everyone knew they were looking at Darren Huckerby, who was now a regular in an Imps shirt. They left at half-time and it was fairly clear it wasn't because they were disappointed.

Lincoln had dispensed with Sam Ellis as manager by then and his replacement, Steve Wicks, hadn't lasted long under John Reames either. A couple of days after the game, new manager John Beck did the deal and Huckerby became a Newcastle player. The transfer fee for a youngster Keith had brought in and developed netted his old club around £500,000, including some easily achievable appearance add-ons. It was also agreed that United would visit Sincil Bank for a pre-season friendly which was worth another £100,000 or so. Keith might have been forgiven for thinking there was no justice, but he didn't let it get to him. Not for long anyway.

Mansfield struggled to keep away from the bottom of the division leading up to the Christmas period. After Holland and a couple of other star players had moved on, King tried anything to refresh the team and pick up a few vital points. In early January 1996, he even picked Keith again, hoping his coach's experience might calm the younger players down if they found the pressure a bit too much. Keith therefore made his debut that season, coming on late in the game against Exeter City at Field Mill. In injury-time, Keith was tackled and he stayed down. Barry Statham, the club physio, dashed straight on, followed shortly by the club doctor, then by the St John's Ambulance volunteers carrying a stretcher. It became clear to everyone that Keith was seriously hurt and after the game news filtered through that his leg was broken. His career as a professional player was finally over.

"After the match, Barry rang and kept saying 'Keith's hurt but don't worry, don't worry,'" Helen recalled. "And the more he said it without telling me what had happened, the more I worried. He then said both his tibia and fibia were broken but he'd be alright. I was so upset."

When Keith left hospital, his leg was in a full-length plaster cast and he couldn't move. If he did, the pain was unbearable. He couldn't even get out of bed. Helen was expecting their first child and, a couple of days after Keith got home, some problems developed with the pregnancy. Keith's natural instinct was to jump out of bed and drive her to hospital but try as he might he couldn't even get upright, so painful was his injury. He eventually gave in and they rang for an ambulance. After a few hours lying helpless on the bed worrying what was wrong and what was happening at the hospital, he was hugely relieved when Helen returned and confirmed the panic was over. Everything was fine.

After a short period at home, Keith wanted to go back to work. The consultant said he was to convalesce for much longer, but he had started to hobble about and he was frustrated. A reserve side and a youth squad were no good without a coach. Rules and Keith Alexander never always saw eye to eye either. He decided drastic action was needed so shuffled outside and into the garage to look for his tools. After sawing off half his plaster cast, he was pleased his movement was improved as a result. He then persuaded Helen to take him to Newark each morning and arranged for Barry Statham to pick him up from there to complete the other half of the journey to Mansfield. He might have to sit down most of the time, but he was back working with players and, to Keith at that time, that was all that mattered.

Except to Keith, in the long term, it wasn't. Coaching and working with players was very important, but he'd had a taste of management and he wanted more. He knew he could do it and he wanted to prove it to everyone else.

*****

Over at Ilkeston, two men sat in an office either side of a desk talking about their football club. Their team wasn't doing well and they needed to decide on a plan of action. One man, Tony Cuthbert, was an Ilkeston Town stalwart. He'd played for them for sixteen years, including a spell as player-manager in the mid '80s, and had been club secretary for the last nine. Facing him was a large, overweight even, round-faced man speaking in a broad Derbyshire accent. Paul Millership was chairman of the club and, as owner of Manor House Furnishing, a local company that supplied Ikea and employed over 1,500 people, he was used to getting what he wanted. He was by far the biggest employer in the Ilkeston area but, after triple bypass heart surgery, was looking to retire and devote his time to his other passion, Ilkeston Town. He'd bought the club in 1989 and built them a new stadium, the New Manor Ground, which was opened in August 1992.

His first manager had been Kenny Burns, the former Nottingham Forest and Scotland defender. The club president was a pretty high-profile individual too. Robert Lindsay, the actor, was born in the town in 1949 and he was a big fan. Once, just before Ilkeston were about to go out and kick-off against Barry Fry's Barnet in the latter stages of the FA Trophy, he burst into the Robins dressing room. As the star of Citizen Smith, the '70s hit sit-com, he threw himself fully into character as Wolfie and gave them an emotional morale-boosting team talk. He even finished by thrusting his arm upwards in salute and shouting "Power to the people!" before turning and striding out again.

Ilkeston had finished runners-up in the Beazer Homes Midland Division the previous season and gained promotion to the Premier League. Millership was putting plenty of his money into the club and he wasn't happy that they looked like going straight back down again. He soon decided that current manager Leighton James, the former Burnley and Wales winger, would have to go. Instead of another 'name' manager, Millership told Cuthbert it was time they got in a younger guy, one who was starting out. They wanted someone who could bring in youngsters who wouldn't just be there for the pay and in the longer term might even raise some cash if they were spotted and sold to bigger clubs. That way, the chairman's money might not be going out in only one direction. Cuthbert had already heard that Andy King's assistant was doing a good job at Field Mill and they both thought he'd fit the bill. He rang Keith and a meeting was arranged.

Chairman Millership was instantly impressed. As a blunt straight-talking businessman he couldn't be doing with waffle. Keith said what he had to say and didn't waste their time talking for ever and saying nothing like a lot of candidates might. Millership told Cuthbert he had heard enough and, not being a lover of red tape, terms and conditions and paperwork, sent him out of the room so he and Keith could do the deal.

"When Keith told me what Ilkeston were offering, I just said go for it," said King. "I didn't want him to go, but they were offering him much more than he was on at Mansfield, even though they were three or four leagues below us."

It wasn't long before Keith worked out his new boss. He was larger than life and he shouted out his orders loud and clear. He was ambitious and driven and he expected everyone at Ilkeston to work as hard as he did. But his bark was worse than his bite and he was scrupulously fair to employees who put in the effort. Millership was well known for his dislike of regulations but Cuthbert put his foot down when it came to football administration. Keith started by bringing in one or two new players, like young Franny Green from Nottingham who he'd had his eye on for some time, and the club secretary saw that the deals were done properly. Keith also registered himself as a player, just in case, and it showed that even though he was nearly forty, he still hadn't given up on playing maybe just a couple more games.

Keith had enough funds to bring in an assistant and he knew of someone who would be ideal. Gary Simpson had been player-manager at Gainsborough Trinity but, because of limited funds, had left to set up a business venture. Keith was aware that Simpson knew the non-league scene like the back of his hand. The two joined forces for the first time and they soon became a very effective managerial team. In those first few weeks, the chairman and manager were also developing what was to turn out to be a great working relationship. They had their fall-outs and Millership insisted on calling Keith 'Huggy' after the character in Starsky and Hutch, the television programme, but despite these negatives, the positives were there for everyone connected with the club to see.

In his first match in charge, Keith saw his team lose 3-0 at Dorchester, their nineteenth game without a win. One week later, after some hard work was done on the training ground and some home truths said off it, the players responded by beating Hastings 1-0 at the New Manor Ground. Keith had recruited his old pal, Jim Kabia, who led the line up front and instantly improved their attacking potential. Then Ilkeston lost at Burton Albion, with Keith getting a booking for protesting at a couple of poor refereeing decisions. If his team was going down, it wouldn't be because of a lack of fight or because they accepted it when things went against them.

Over at Mansfield, a famous name was being written on the official team sheet. Daley Thompson had won decathalon gold for Great Britain in the 1980 and 1984 Olympics. He'd retired from athletics in 1992 and had fancied himself as a footballer, despite his advancing years. Stamford Town had fancied him, too, and he'd done well, scoring seven goals in twelve games. He moved to Field Mill and, after a few reserve games, made it on to the subs bench for the first team. Keith knew Thompson, having met him in St Lucia where he was doing some athletics coaching, and thought he'd give Ilkeston some steel in defence if he could persuade him to sign up and play at centre-half. He did indeed sign and went on to play nine games as the Robins battled to stay in the top division.

Thompson was never one to conform. He famously attended the BBC Sports Personality of the Year awards in 1982 wearing a track suit when everyone else was dressed to the nines. He compounded his faux pas ten-fold when, having been declared the winner, he began his acceptance speech to the whole nation by saying: "I feel like a shit." Thankfully this wasn't meant as an immediate physical need, more an admission that he knew he wasn't dressed appropriately, but it was an awful moment nonetheless. This lack of discipline revealed itself again, albeit on a smaller scale, when, during the return league game at Ilkeston, Jason Rhodes of Burton pulled him down. Thompson got up and head-butted the striker, who was out cold before he hit the deck. The referee showed what was probably the most straightforward red card he'd ever awarded, but Ilkeston, with ten men, never gave up and snatched a late winner to earn three valuable points.

As Keith and Gary worked tirelessly trying to improve their team's performances, news filtered through about another of the manager's former pupils. At nearby Derby County, defender Matt Carbon had agreed a deal that benefited his old club, Lincoln City, to the tune of £375,000. Again the irony wasn't lost on Keith that a club could sack their manager and then reap the rewards of his labours for years to come, but that's football. Anyway he was enjoying his new challenge and he hadn't got time to think about what might have been.

Despite some improved results the Robins had too much ground to make up and a 3-1 defeat by Gloucester City in the penultimate game of the season saw relegation confirmed. Paul Millership was disappointed his team hadn't stayed up but he was more disappointed that he hadn't got his new manager on board sooner. He was impressed with him, he liked him and he was optimistic that his beloved club would soon be back up there with him in charge.

For a club that was used to entertaining teams like Halesowen Town, VS Rugby and Merthyr Tydfil, the summer of 1996 saw some very different visitors gracing the playing surface at the New Manor Ground. The Euro '96 tournament was being held in England, and Portugal, who were to play their group games in the East Midlands, were keen to find some training facilities where they could practise behind closed doors. Ilkeston Town, and Paul Millership in particular, were not backwards at coming forwards in volunteering their ground and the Derbyshire FA were persuaded to back them as their generous offer was considered by the English and Portuguese football authorities. And so it was that Rui Costa, Paulo Sousa, Joao Pinto, Luis Figo and the rest of the Portugal squad trained hard on set-plays and dead-ball routines on the Robins pitch before going into battle with Italy, Holland and France.

Keith sat in the stand and observed every session. He got Tony Cuthbert to persuade the Portugal officials to allow a few Ilkeston fans into the ground to watch a couple of times too. He thought it was a once-in-a-lifetime opportunity to watch the great Eusebio coaching some of the most skilful players he'd seen in the flesh and it was only fair that some supporters should enjoy it too. During one training session, Keith watched as groups of players gathered at each of the corner flags at one end of the ground. One by one they placed the ball in the quadrant, stepped back and pinged it high over the goalmouth to within inches of the flag the other side. There, a team-mate, without having to move hardly a muscle, would casually trap it under the sole of his boot. This went on for fifteen minutes, with balls flying from one side to the other, all landing accurately and being controlled with ease.

Keith had already picked up a few new warm-up routines from the Portugal squad and he introduced them when his own players turned up for pre-season training in the evening, after they'd finished work. One night, after a heavy fitness session, he decided it wouldn't do any harm to get them to try the 'corner-to-corner' routine and see what they could do. He explained it to them and left them to it. He stood there watching impassively, arms folded, as footballs flew into the stand, bobbled along the ground or disappeared into the car park. That one episode confirmed to Keith once more what he'd already learned at Lincoln. If you want results, it's no good trying to get players to do what they can't. On the contrary, you need to work on what they're good at. If that means developing strength, pace and determination because that's what they already have, then get on with it. You can make a team out of that, a winning team, and if a bit of skill follows, then so much the better.

Keith and Gary knew that a lot of the squad had to be moved on and they set about recruiting better players. The chairman was more than willing to back them financially so they enjoyed being part of a club that was one of the highest spenders in their league. This was a new experience for both of them. Jim Kabia was given a new deal and Scott Huckerby was brought in. The younger brother of Darren had already had his potential seen by Keith.

"Scott hasn't got as much pace as Darren," Keith said. "But he has more tricks up his sleeve and has a lot of skill."

The squad was assembled and the players were worked hard. They trained in the evenings and a series of friendlies were arranged. One night they were working on attack versus defence when a loud noise was heard overhead. It grew and grew until it became deafening. Then they became engulfed in a shadow that got bigger and darker and a blustering gale that grew stronger. At the last minute the players, Keith and Gary all scattered as a helicopter landed in the centre circle. A beaming Paul Millership climbed out, only to be greeted by Keith who berated him for, if not killing someone, then scaring them all to death.

"It's my ground and my fucking helicopter," the chairman

replied, "I'll park the fucking thing where I want!"

Keith contacted Andy King and a friendly against Mansfield was set up. Work was being done at Field Mill and the New Manor Ground was having alterations carried out to meet new regulations. The friendly was therefore to take place at nearby Southwell's ground. After the game, King, Keith, Gary and Tony Cuthbert went across to the Saracen's Head in the middle of town to unwind. King bought the first round and the group sat down and chatted about life in their respective football circles. Then the Mansfield manager reminded Keith that it was his turn to get the beers in. Before he could leave his chair, Keith was told to sit still by Tony who said he'd get the round out of the club's drinks kitty. He took an envelope stuffed full of twenty pound notes out of his pocket and went over to the bar. Andy King, who'd played at the highest level, coached and managed for years, and thought he'd seen everything in the game, couldn't contain his surprise.

"A drinks kitty!" he exclaimed. "I'm in charge of a Football League club and I haven't got a bean to spend. Kit, balls, you name it – I can't get it. And you're non-league and you've even got a fucking drinks kitty!"

The season got underway and Ilkeston made a steady start. Unlike previous seasons, it became clear that the club was united from top to bottom. Keith spoke to the fans and made them feel part of what he was trying to achieve. He impressed on the non-playing staff how important they were. Millership started to involve his son, Alex, in the running of the club, and Keith's sons, Matthew and Paul, were often at the ground when matches were being played or training was taking place. They enjoyed spending time with their dad and they especially liked the way he involved them while he was working. Cuthbert's two sons, Lee and Ryan, were big fans too and were delighted when Keith told them they were welcome to travel on the team coach when they wanted to watch the Robins play away. After home games the chairman laid on food and drinks for everyone, all at his own expense, and they all enjoyed some terrific nights. If anyone needed to know the benefit of building a team ethic at a football club, then little Ilkeston Town in the 1996-97 season could teach them a thing or two.

The Robins could do no wrong on their travels and didn't lose an away game until December. It was a different matter at home where their form was the main reason they were only mid-table halfway through the season. Then Keith and Gary's hard work suddenly bore fruit and the team started to win regularly at home and away. Huckerby and Kabia scored at will and Ilkeston won twelve and drew three in their last fifteen games. A 4-0 win at Stafford Rangers at the end of April was spoiled, however, when news filtered through that Rothwell Town had scraped a 3-2 victory at Sutton Coldfield and had pipped them for promotion. It had been a good season nevertheless and everyone at the club had enjoyed it. At the end-of-season awards night, all the talk was of Keith taking them one step further next time round.

Keith attended another presentation evening soon after when he was invited over as guest of honour to the Cliftonville Player of the Year dinner at the Europa Hotel in Belfast. They hoped he'd be able to take in their last game of the season against Crusaders that afternoon but his plane was delayed and he missed the match. At six o'clock, he rang the organisers to say he was just about to board the plane and he'd see them at the dinner. By the time he arrived the main course had been served. As he walked to his table, over 300 guests stopped eating and gave him a standing ovation. Keith normally dealt with situations, whether good or bad, in a laid back calm sort of way, but he was genuinely surprised and moved by the reception he got that evening. He had played only nine games for the club and it was a measure of the respect and affection they'd instantly felt towards their import from across the water.

Ilkeston fans were right to be optimistic. The 1997-98 season saw their side score a hundred and twenty-three goals in forty league games. The fast direct football Keith's team produced got results and the chairman was delighted to see his club attract their biggest gates for over thirty years. Promotion was gained and only an exceptional Grantham team stopped Ilkeston winning the Southern League Midland Division title. They won it by one point, even though the Robins finished the season with an astounding plus eighty four goal difference. Whilst promotion had been the first priority, a run in the FA Cup had been a thrilling diversion. In the first round, 2,504 fans packed into the New Manor Ground to see Keith mastermind a 2-1 win over his former club, Boston United. In the second round, the manager's profile was lifted significantly when his team drew at Scunthorpe 1-1 and the highlights were shown that night on Match of the Day. Sadly for Keith, the Football League side triumphed 2-1 in the replay, which meant Ilkeston missed out on a glamorous third round tie with Crystal Palace of the Premier League.

The step up to the Southern League Premier Division the following season looked like being a tough one. Ilkeston would be facing bigger clubs with better players in front of larger crowds. They needn't have worried. Keith and Gary's methods soon made their illustrious opponents take notice and their players were now adding skill and guile to their up-and-at-'em style of play. Life at Ilkeston was never dull though. One morning, a member of the ground-staff arrived to find the gates had been forced open and was astounded to see a number of gypsy caravans parked on the pitch. Their occupants seemed to have made themselves firmly at home in their new surroundings. His protests were met with a not unexpectedly abrupt response. The chairman was not inclined to deal with the matter through the submission of paperwork to the authorities or by entering into a long drawn-out legal process.

Some time ago it had been alleged, although never proved, that one of his 'assistants' had appeared on the Cook Report, an ITV investigative programme that examined various dubious business practices. Whoever arranged it would never be established, but the new residents at the home of Ilkeston Town Football Club were soon sent on their way when a number of very big men turned up. They invited them to pick up all their refuse, pack their bags and tow their caravans to anywhere as long as it was somewhere else, which they duly did.

Nuneaton Borough were the pace-setters in the league but Ilkeston and Boston United gave them a run for their money for as long as they could. In the end, the Robins finished third behind their Lincolnshire opponents on goal difference, both of them lagging a long way behind Borough. Keith had led his side to the highest ever league position in their history.

Good management doesn't involve being satisfied with past achievements. The aim must be to improve and, if you've already done well, to do even better. Consequently Keith and Gary approached the 1999-00 season looking to take little Ilkeston Town into the Conference, the highest level of non-league football. Keith recruited Ian Helliwell to lead the line up front. He was a big target man and had made over 300 Football League appearances, so he fitted the bill perfectly. The first half of the season saw Keith and his team do well and they managed to keep in touch with league leaders Boston United. In the preliminary rounds of the FA Cup, they couldn't stop scoring goals – beating Solihull Borough 4-3, Wingate 5-0 and Romford 3-0. They gained another Football League scalp in the first round proper, beating Carlisle at the New Manor Ground. A crowd of over 2,500 at Ilkeston watched them draw with Rushden and Diamonds and they lost the replay to miss out on a third round fixture with Sheffield United.

In January, Keith signed three new players. They all arrived from Matlock and they were all related. Stephen Heath was a former England youth international, his brother Billy had started out at Hull City and another brother, Mike, had been on Spurs' books. Although all three had made good starts to their football careers, they hadn't achieved much since and had played for a great many non-league clubs. Despite knowing each other well, they didn't add a lot to the team ethic and they all departed after making only thirteen appearances between them. Keith needed to strengthen the side to maintain the momentum but, for once, he wasn't given a lot more funds. Results became mixed and the Robins' promotion challenge faltered. They finished ninth, a long way behind champions Boston United, and Keith was very disappointed his side had fallen away in the second half of the season.

As the next season approached, it became clear things had changed a bit. Millership was less willing to fund the club to the same degree and was keen that Alex, his son, took a more prominent role. He remained as chairman but, whether for health or financial reasons, felt he needed to relax his grip. Consequently the squad, far from being strengthened to go for the title again, was weakened when one or two influential players were tempted to move elsewhere. Alex was seen more at the ground and he struck up a friendship with Matthew, Keith's eldest son.

"I'd passed my driving test," said Matthew. "And dad sorted me out my first car. It was a beaten up old Ford Escort but I was as proud as punch with it. I turned up at Ilkeston to watch the team train and coincidentally Alex also arrived in the car park in his new car. It was his first car, too, and his dad had treated him to a brand new Porsche 911. I still loved the car my dad had got me!"

The team got off to an inconsistent start and it became clear that this was going to be a transitional season. Keith, as shown by his tendency to move a lot as a player and by his reaction to his Lincoln sacking, constantly assessed his position, even if it seemed he had got a good job at that particular time. He would always think about the next step, whether his current club was doing well or doing badly. Stability could never be guaranteed in the football industry so he'd try and be one step ahead. As much as he could anyway.

As winter set in, Keith finally decided he'd taken Ilkeston as far as he could. He'd had offers from other clubs and it was time for a new challenge. He broke the news to Millership senior, who took it very badly. He didn't explode or rant and rave like he did a lot of the time. He was just upset because Keith had meant everything to him. Father and son Millership searched for a new manager, deciding to go back to the old approach by appointing a 'name', and John McGovern, the former Nottingham Forest and Scotland midfielder, was brought in. But Paul didn't have the same enthusiasm and it became clear his heart was no longer in it.

Keith had been Ilkeston Town's most successful manager in their history. They'd played two hundred and fifty-three games under him and had won one hundred and thirty three, drawn sixty, and lost sixty; a pretty good record. But his statistics at a modest non-league club weren't the most significant thing about his time there. It was his policy of bonding every single person at a little club into a complete team so that they could achieve success and have a good time doing so. A lot of much bigger clubs could and should learn from that. And it was his relationship with a chairman who was almost the total opposite in terms of personality and manner.

"Mr Millership used to come up to me after a game in the clubhouse," said Matthew. "The drinks had been flowing a bit and he'd be merry, to say the least. He'd put an arm round me like he wanted to confide in me about something and say 'I fucking love your dad, I really do'."

Things never stay the same in football though. It was time to move on.

7

The Drill Field, Back at the Bank with Buckley, Failing Finances

"Lincoln City hang to life by a thread. I am not prepared to be the person who cuts that thread"
Judge Alistair Norris QC

"It was a Tuesday night game and the caretaker-manager had put me back in the team. We'd heard Keith Alexander and Gary Simpson were in the crowd looking at us so I was pleased I got both our goals," said Gary Fletcher, later to become Gary Taylor-Fletcher and play in the Premier League with Blackpool. "Before he was sacked, manager Mark Gardiner used to pick me and if I didn't score I'd be dropped after two games. Then the other strikers wouldn't score either and I'd be back in. I was only a young lad and being in and out of the team all the time put too much pressure on me to score. I'd fluff a chance and my head would drop."

Keith and Gary were impressed with the striker and, after checking out the team a couple of times and looking into the set-up behind the scenes, weren't unimpressed with the offer to take over at Northwich Victoria. It was a few steps up from Ilkeston and only one rung lower than the Football League. Keith became their first full-time manager, so impressed were the board with him, and he beat off other candidates like John Beck and Paul Futcher. The only problem was it was October 2000, and the Vics were already five points adrift at the bottom of the Conference. They'd only won two games since August. If a new manager couldn't bring about a speedy revival then relegation was definitely on the cards. As it was, Keith saw enough of the club and its potential at that midweek game to encourage him to agree a deal and sign a contract. He needed a new challenge and this certainly fitted the bill.

Formed in 1874, Northwich Victoria were named after the reigning monarch of the time. Their home, The Drill Field, was thought, by people in Northwich at any rate, to be the world's oldest football ground. A few years earlier the club had arranged a series of functions and events to recognise this historic claim, only for a couple of less than loyal local historians to dispute it and spoil the celebrations a little bit. The board of directors were now more interested in celebrating a few wins, so they watched anxiously as their new manager got stuck into the task before him.

"As soon as he started, Keith took me to one side," said Fletcher. "He said I'd be in the team as long as I worked hard and forgot about having to take every chance that came my way. He told me that I was good enough to play every game and if I didn't score, it didn't matter because I'd probably create enough goals for other people. We'd got some good players there, like Mark Bailey and Adie Mike. He told us that we were all too good to be where we were but we'd lost our way a bit. He gave us a way to play and we suddenly all knew what we were supposed to be doing."

Keith introduced his trademark 5-2-3 formation and the players found a new belief. The football was direct but only when it needed to be. A long ball would be played out of defence to break up an opposition attack but it wasn't aimless. Far from it, as a striker ran into the channel and then ran at the opposing defenders. Team-mates would be quick to support him and chances would be created through good attacking football.

"Keith didn't just show us how to play," confirmed Fletcher. "He picked the right characters. He didn't want fancy-dans or arrogant so-and-sos in the team. He wanted us to get on, whether it was on or off the pitch. A proper team."

The Alexander effect was instant. In their next five games Northwich won four and drew one. Any sort of victory looked a million miles off before he took over, and they beat Doncaster, Woking, Kettering and Dagenham and Redbridge in quick succession as soon as he arrived. The Vics had been drawn away to Bury in the first round of the FA Cup and their new-found form earned them a 1-1 draw. An Adie Mike goal was enough to give them victory in the replay and Northwich had secured their first Football League scalp in seventeen years. In the second round they entertained Leyton Orient and at 2-0 down they looked to be heading out of the competition. A superb fight back saw them lead 3-2 with Fletcher scoring two and Mike one. Only a late equaliser prevented another giant-killing.

"At 2-0 up it should have been all over," said Orient manager Tommy Taylor. "But Northwich put us under enormous pressure and I'm pleased we came away still in the competition."

The replay was shown live on Sky Sports. The draw for the third round had taken place and the winners would be at home to Spurs. What was already a tasty fixture suddenly had a whole lot more riding on it. Keith's instructions were followed to the letter and the Vics were 2-0 up after only eleven minutes. Maybe they'd gained an advantage too early because it gave the hosts plenty of time to recover, and recover they did. They pulled one back and then equalised just before the final whistle. Orient nicked the winner in extra-time and the cup adventure was over. But Keith's reputation as a manager was growing and the television coverage enhanced it. Of course, a lot of people in the game already knew him. They could now see he was a promising manager who knew how to use resources well and build a team that got results. That live TV game revealed him to a much wider audience and the Alexander stock grew still further.

In December, Northwich made the long journey to Yeovil for a league fixture. Delighted with the team's performances and the income from the cup games, the board had agreed that the team and staff could have an overnight stay – something that the finances never normally allowed. They left Northwich in a downpour and the wet weather didn't subside during the whole journey. As they arrived at their hotel, word was that the pitch at Huish Park, Yeovil's home ground, was waterlogged. Keith made a couple of calls and was assured that there was no chance of the game being played.

There was little point in returning home that night so it was decided they'd book into their rooms, have a relaxing evening, train locally in the morning and then travel back after lunch. The hotel was large with various bars and function rooms. After the Northwich contingent had found the dining room and enjoyed a pleasant evening meal, it became clear from the amount of smartly dressed people that were arriving that several companies were holding their Christmas parties there that night. The players looked on enviously and asked their manager if they were allowed to have a few beers before they went to their rooms. Keith knew that he wouldn't have another 'Torquay-gate' on his hands because he'd already been reliably informed that the opposition's pitch was unplayable, so he granted their wish. In fact he and Gary joined them for a couple of rounds before leaving them to it. As he left, Keith told his players that they'd better behave themselves and they needed to be in bed at a reasonable time.

Hours later, the sound of booming music could still be heard and Keith woke up. Squinting at his watch in the darkness he saw that it was almost three o'clock. He thought he'd better check that none of his squad had been tempted by the revelry and missed his curfew. Keith didn't see why it was only up to him to be the players' guardian so he woke up Gary and told him to help. A few minutes later the two of them sheepishly entered the room where the music and merriment was at its loudest. They were greeted by the sight of the whole Northwich playing squad interspersed with office girls, middle-aged executives and other staggering guests in a conga line snaking in and out of tables and across the dance floor. One or two of the players noticed that their manager and his assistant had appeared. Expecting an almighty rollicking, they watched as Keith looked at Gary, shrugged, reached over and grabbed a party hat from a table close by, put it on, and joined the end of the conga line, kicking out his enormously long legs in time to the music.

Yeovil were top of the Conference because they'd got good players and a good manager. They were well organised, too, and were looking forward to beating lowly Northwich Victoria to maintain their 100 per cent home record in front of a large crowd of loyal fans. Such were their organisational skills, a large number of volunteers turned up at Huish Park, probably not that long after the time their opponents were crawling off to bed, armed with forks and buckets. A bit of wet weather wasn't going to stop their pursuit of the league title, even if most sensible people thought they were wasting their time. Hours later, when the referee arrived, he must have felt he needed to reward the club and the legion of helpers for all their hard work because, amazingly, he declared the still sodden pitch playable.

If the Northwich squad felt rough early next morning after their night on the tiles, they felt even worse when news of his decision reached their hotel. As it was, they roused themselves and gave the home side their toughest game yet on their own pitch. Whilst other better prepared and, it has to be said, un-hungover opponents had been brushed aside all season, Northwich battled all the way and lost only to a solitary goal. It was still a defeat but one of only a few under Keith's leadership. It was also a measure of the team ethic he had engendered that they could compete so well under such difficult, albeit self-inflicted, circumstances.

Playing regularly under Keith's leadership had benefited Gary Fletcher as well as the team as a whole. He was scoring goals and attracting interest. He soon found out that a good manager doesn't just sign players and pick the team. He has to look after the club too and if that means making the best of your assets, then so be it. Fletcher was working in a hotel at Widnes and found work as a barman in Warrington too. He only got £50 per week with the Vics, with a modest goal bonus enhancing this meagre wage. Keith knew Stoke City had been watching him and rumour had it an Aston Villa scout had been lurking about at a recent game. He took his player to one side and said he should be on a much better deal at the Drill Field. As luck would have it, Keith had seen the chairman that day and a new contract was ready and waiting for him. Fletcher knew he was getting some good reviews but didn't know such high-profile clubs had been checking him out.

He agreed the deal and then, when the phone started ringing with some tasty offers, realised that anyone who wanted him would have to pay Northwich a whole lot more than they would have needed to a couple of weeks earlier. Fletcher was far from critical of his gaffer, though. He knew that good managers did that sort of thing routinely. If he moved somewhere big, he'd be able to play full-time in front of large crowds and he'd be on a wage he could only have dreamed of at the start of the season. His old club would have the money to spend on maybe four good players for next season and be able to clear a bit of debt for good measure. Unfortunately, Fletcher sustained a bad injury just at the wrong time and was unable to play for three months. Even so, as soon as the player was back training, Keith told him Bolton Wanderers wanted him to train with them for a week with a view to signing him. As a part-time player who wasn't match fit, Fletcher's spell at Bolton wasn't a success and he wasn't able to impress them. Then he went on a month's loan to Hull City but his lack of fitness let him down again. Finally, Leyton Orient, a team Fletcher had run ragged a few times in the cup games, made an offer and he signed for them. Northwich got a £75,000 fee so everyone, including Keith Alexander, was happy.

The team had performed much better under their new manager and the final league table saw them finish in

A proud captain – Elms Junior School Under 11s

A goal-scorer and winner at Wembley with Stamford in
the FA Vase final in 1980

A youthful Keith shows off his FA Vase winners medal

Starring for the Mariners in the late 80s

The Mariners and THAT fish!

An Imps player in 1990

Playing for the Imps.
Holding the ball up
to bring others into
the game

First taste of management.
Boss of Lincoln City 1993-94

Second in command with Alan Buckley at Lincoln City in 2001

The new manager with the shoestring squad that confounded
the critics in 2002-03

Made it! Celebrating making the play-offs with the Imps in 2003

Keith and the two Garys take in the Millennium Stadium

The Lincoln City play-off squad

Leading them out

Taking in the play-off final atmosphere

Lucky yellow socks

Keith and Gary look out of the Guildhall windows to greet the fans below at a civic reception in 2003

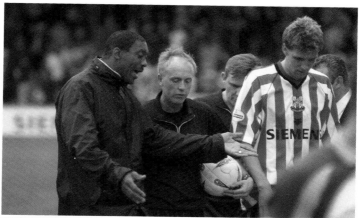

Not seeing eye to eye.
Keith makes his feelings
known to the officials

At ease with the media

Lincoln City's Simon
Yeo shows his support
for his stricken gaffer
after scoring against
Bristol Rovers

A return to football. Keith walks out in his first match back after
serious illness in 2004

Going back to Cardiff.
Play-off success away
at Macclesfield

Getting the
message across

Keith and the author – renewing his contract at Lincoln City

Manager of the month with the Imps in March 2006

With Gordon Banks at
a fundraising dinner

Opening of The Goal community facility at Sincil Bank

Coaching and developing

Keith with Barry Fry as he joins the Posh in May 2006

The Macclesfield Town squad 2009-10

Keith with sons Matt and Paul

seventeenth spot. Their results in April and May had been excellent and the club that had been odds-on favourites for the drop at the end of 2000 had avoided it with games to spare the following spring. Everything at home was rosy, too, with Keith and Helen now married. Their ceremony had taken place in Dunholme church with John Cockerill acting as best man and their little boy, Jack, looking on.

While Keith had been orchestrating a great escape in Cheshire, a former boss had been doing the same at a former club back in Lincolnshire. With sixteen games to go, Alan Buckley was quickly recruited by the new board of directors at League Two Lincoln City. They were also rock-solid favourites for the relegation trapdoor. Ten of those games were away and the Imps hadn't managed a win on their travels all season. Buckley, like Keith, had an instant impact and the team won his first three games in charge, including a stirring home victory against Cardiff City who were top of the table. Results were mixed after that but enough points were gathered to avoid relegation. Once the league programme was concluded, Buckley reflected that he needed a good assistant if things were to be done properly and professionally next season. He had a short list of two or three and he was determined that one of them would join him at Sincil Bank as soon as possible.

*****

Having been chairman for a short turbulent time, I was pleased we had Alan Buckley on board. He'd got a good track record and, as we looked forward to next season, we recognised he'd already done an excellent job by keeping us in the Football League. We were keen to back him as he built a better team, and that included his request to have a capable assistant. Buckley asked about Paul Groves but Grimsby wanted him to stay. He was their skipper and it sounded like he was being thought of as a future manager at Blundell Park. Buckley then sounded out John Cockerill, or 'Cockers' as he called him, but he too was under contract with the Mariners. Finally, a certain Keith Alexander was mentioned. We approved of this, to say the least, and a couple of days after the players reported back for pre-season training in mid-July, Keith was tempted away from Northwich and appointed as Director of Coaching, tasked to oversee the development of the Centre of Excellence, youth team and pro-football squad. Buckley stated that Keith was specifically instructed to make sure that the manager's distinctive passing style of play was adopted and improved at all levels of the club. Full of bravado and optimism, I remember telling the local newspaper reporter that I thought we'd got the best management team in the division. Goalkeeper Alan Marriott already knew a little bit about Keith.

"I was in digs when I first came to Lincoln and I shared with a lad called Anthony Henry," said Marriott. "He was struggling at Lincoln and Keith wanted him to sign for Northwich. He'd ring him and tell him how a step down and playing regular games might resurrect his career. As soon as Keith started at Lincoln we liked him. He was laid back and easy going. He was fairly quiet at first but we soon knew he was someone we could talk to. He was a good go-between between us and Alan Buckley."

For all the optimism for the season ahead, the first team's style of play and the results they achieved could be summed up in one word – disappointing. Or, from a chairman's perspective, probably better in two words – bloody disappointing. Lincoln never went more than three games unbeaten in League Two. The passing game didn't work. We looked great in the middle third of the pitch but we couldn't score in the attacking third and couldn't defend in the back one. We'd play lovely approach football but then a tough-looking defender or midfielder would clatter one of our guys, whack the ball forward and another tough nut playing up front would harass our defence and be through on goal. We were never anywhere near the automatic promotion places, the play-off places or, for that matter, the top half. We spent most of the season hoping we'd sneak enough points to keep relegation at bay and even then it was Halifax Town who saved us by being so poor and being cast adrift at the bottom.

The first team squad were nearly all late twenty or thirty-somethings and while they could play a bit, none of them was fast, strong, or could battle. Mark Bailey came in from Northwich as recommended to Buckley by Keith, but generally untried non-league prospects with potential weren't the manager's favourite type of player. It was the same with youngsters too. Keith worked hard with John Schofield, the head of the Centre of Excellence, and some good young propects were being developed. Lee Frecklington was looking very promising and would go on to make a name for himself at Lincoln and Peterborough. But none of the youth squad was introduced into the first team, Buckley stubbornly preferring 'ready-made' professionals.

The 'disappointing' theme continued in cup competitions too, with Lincoln going out of all three early on with barely a whimper. The only highlight of the cup games, which probably represented the only highlight of the season as a whole, was an FA Cup first round replay at Gigg Lane against Bury. After a 1-1 draw after extra-time, it all came down to a penalty shoot-out. With the scores level, up stepped ex-soldier Dave Cameron with a chance to win it for City. Cameron was a big slow target man and his touch was sometimes rudimentary, but he led the line like his life depended on it and he was a real fans' favourite. He beat the keeper with a low shot into the corner and Lincoln were through. He lifted the front of his shirt over his head and ran, arms aloft, to the fans to celebrate, to hug them as they reached over the fence and to milk their acclaim. Except he had forgotten, or couldn't see, in which bit of the ground the visiting Imps fans were housed and he'd run straight towards a large contingent of home supporters in the opposite direction. Hearing their abuse and then setting off for the correct part of the stadium didn't have quite the same impact, but that moment of minor triumph and major amusement was a very enjoyable exception in a dirge of a season.

As the team struggled on the pitch, the new team in the boardroom were struggling too. We spent months trying to sort out the finances of the club, the full extent of the debt we inherited became known and the poor results meant attendances were low which made things worse. To put the tin hat on it, the Football League deal with ITV Digital went belly-up and the loss of a projected £180,000 chunk of income turned out to be the straw that broke the camel's back. As we tried to keep a professional profile publicly, behind the scenes all manner of things were going on to try and address the club's financial turmoil. Needless to say, rumours leaked out about the difficulties. The local paper reported that we couldn't afford to pay a Powergen bill of £10,000 and that the electricity was going to be turned off. 'Lights To Go Out On City' was the headline, pretty predictably.

Four games before the end of the season, we confirmed that the pro-football staff hadn't been paid on time, and when they were, it wasn't in full. It was only a loan from the Professional Footballers' Association that helped make this happen. Keith and Helen now had a baby daughter, Jenny, and had moved to a larger house in Dunholme. The pleasure they'd felt at Keith being back working near home was seriously spoiled by his wages not appearing in the bank as expected. Then the paper reported we couldn't afford the cost of the team bus for our last game at Hull and the team would be travelling in cars. I quickly refuted this claim, saying that we might have problems but we'd operate professionally until they'd been solved. It was only a sponsor who stumped up the money for the bus that made sure my assurances were accurate.

Finally, we came clean and confirmed that the club was in trouble and we'd brought in Begbies Traynor, insolvency practitioners, to help us. They'd submitted a petition for an administration order to the High Court on our behalf. As our penultimate game of the season at home to Rochdale approached, a huge publicity campaign was launched. I was featured on the front of the *Lincolnshire Echo* Kitchener-style saying 'Your Club Needs You'. We asked for everyone to come to the game to show they wanted their club to survive. A massive fund-raising effort got going with bucket collections, supporter groups' campaigns and donations from sponsors, local businesses, directors and the general public all contributing to a fighting fund. On the day of the game, Lincoln's Member of Parliament, Gillian Merron, led a march of fans and well-wishers through the city to the ground.

Over 6,000 people attended the match and saw us draw 1-1. The result was immaterial, of course, but the day confirmed that everyone was behind our efforts to survive. At Hull I went in the home boardroom for a short time but watched the match with our fans behind the goal. We drew 1-1 again and Alan Buckley and Keith came over with the players after the final whistle to applaud the Imps supporters. Buckley even mimed a simple side-foot chance that Dave Cameron had missed to win the game late on and then, smiling, looked skywards as if to say 'How did he miss it!' This rare show of warmth and humour by the manager made me feel even worse, because, unbeknown to everyone around me and known only by the board, I was due to let him go in two days' time to save the club money.

On the Monday after the game, Buckley walked into the boardroom and sat facing the directors. Before I could start my carefully prepared explanation about him having to go because we couldn't afford his salary, one director laughed and said: "You know what's coming don't you?" I don't think I've ever witnessed a more cringe-worthy few seconds than those that followed. Buckley clearly didn't know what was about to happen and there was no reason he should have done. When our difficulties were explained, our now ex-manager was as gentlemanly as he had been during his time at the club, and he left with good grace and our best wishes. Our chief executive, Dick Chester, was then given the news that he too would have to leave. The only uplifting moment of a thoroughly dark day came when I asked Keith if he was prepared to take over as caretaker-manager.

"Being manager here again might not be a long job if the club is wound up in the High Court," Keith later told the local paper after agreeing to our request. We'd also told him we wanted him to take over as permanent manager if we were successful in the courtroom in Birmingham. He'd be on only the same salary as he was as Buckley's assistant and the playing budget would be slashed, but he agreed he'd do it. Having got to know him over the last year, we were delighted. We just needed a club for him to manage.

On the Friday before our court appearance on the following Monday, Mike Ellingworth, our insolvency guy, came to meet the whole board and handed us each a letter saying that, despite his best efforts, he could not support our application to the court. We were too far gone. This blow was followed by a meeting with two potential investors who we hoped might be our saviours and who turned out to be far from impressive. Desperate as we might have been, we sent them on their way. Sometime later they were recruited by a club in the south west and, putting it as diplomatically as I can, their contribution there subsequently proved to be a complete disaster. We were looking at our club being wound up and the Lincoln City boardroom at the end of an eventful day was a very gloomy place indeed.

Suddenly we got a couple of phone calls from people who wanted to put in some funds and a glimmer of a plan started to come together. Then the Professional Footballers' Association said they could help a little bit. Over the weekend we met the bank and they were starting to look positive too. Prior to our appearance in the High Court in Birmingham, Mike and I met our barrister at his offices nearby. He looked at our financial plan and the pledges of money we'd received, picked holes in it and, minutes before we were due to dash to the court building, wrote out his own version on, I swear, the back of an envelope. He presented it to the court as if it had been prepared for months by a team of highly skilled financial experts.

"Lincoln City, like a lot of small clubs, hangs to life by a thread," said Judge Alistair Norris QC. "I am not prepared to be the person who cuts that thread." I cried when he said that, and was pleased I was sitting facing the bench so that our fans in the public gallery couldn't see me. They cheered at the end of the hearing and sang 'There's only one Lincoln City.' We were allowed a few more days to put things together and, back in the same courtroom on the Friday with our plan now much more solid, the judge confirmed that the situation wasn't the fault of the new board and income was there to underwrite the club's immediate existence. Administration was granted and cost cutting, bringing in new funds and reaching an arrangement with creditors through a Company Voluntary Agreement would be part of the recovery strategy.

One of the many calls I made after the hearing was to tell Keith he was our new manager. He was pleased, just like everyone else, that our little club had a future again.

"We were shocked when Alan left," said Imps goalkeeper and the *Lincolnshire Echo* Star Man of the Season, Alan Marriott, "But Keith is well respected and has a great knowledge of the game. He gets on well with everyone and the fans like him too. He has a lot of experience of lower league players and a lot of contacts. Now we've got through the court hearings, the players and our new manager will want to give something back."

"The way everybody has pulled together has been fantastic," said Keith, when asked about taking over as gaffer only eight days after Alan Buckley's departure. "Every day is a new day and I'll be working hard to put a team together that will cause other clubs some problems next season. We need to be stronger and we need to be more physical. Of course, we'd like to play passing football but sometimes that isn't possible and if we need to mix things up, we will."

Those last few words were very significant. Someone once asked Keith, as assistant manager, what he'd done that morning with the team. "I carried the balls", he'd replied, smiling. On being asked "What else?" he answered: "Nothing. That's it." Local radio reporter and elder statesman at BBC Radio Lincolnshire, the late Mike Molloy, used to interview Buckley and he often felt the assistant manager next to him wasn't totally convinced by what he was hearing. Keith would never criticise Alan Buckley, and he knew that good football was the correct way to play. He would always be fiercely loyal to his former boss, but Keith knew that there were other ways to get results. If his boss hadn't been so set in his ways he might have listened to what he'd said and changed things for the better.

Some of the players at other clubs that Keith kept recommending might have made things happen too, if only they'd been signed and given a chance. Having a collection of nice guys in the team was fine. It was OK having a team spirit that was . . . OK, but it was ten times better to have a squad of characters; ones who would routinely run through a brick wall for their mates and their manager and where the team spirit was worth at least a goal start. If a player could do tricks with the ball that other players could only dream of but was knackered after an hour, he was no good to anyone. If he was a goal-scoring midfielder but hadn't got the legs to get into the opposition box quickly enough, he wasn't much use either. From Keith's early comments on taking on the manager's job, it seemed that the type of football in the 2002-03 season might be a little bit different.

The summer of 2002 had been a turbulent one in the history of Lincoln City. The board, staff, supporters and a huge amount of other people had worked hard to ensure the club's survival. It would take a lot more hard work to make sure the finances recovered still further. The new manager had a lot to do too. He hardly had any players and would have precious little money to buy new ones. The last thing the club would need now would be a relegation battle even though, after all their problems, they'd be favourites for the drop. Of all the challenges facing everyone at Lincoln City, it was Keith Alexander who faced the biggest.

8

Fine Football, Falling Ill

"The only thing we could do was do our best for Keith"
Simon Yeo

Keith Alexander had fairly conventional tastes when it came to relaxing; when he found time for such a thing that is. Like a lot of football people he enjoyed a round of golf. For years, he played right-handed and then, following some advice by a local golf pro, he changed to left-handed and his game improved enormously. When his Lincoln City side had defied the odds and reached the League Two play-off final in 2003, he was mightily impressed that the board agreed that the club should set up base camp at Celtic Manor in Newport because that would be the home of the Ryder Cup in 2010.

After the disappointment of losing to Bournemouth 5-2, he was quick to get over it by resolving that, with a bit of fine tuning and strengthening, his squad could enjoy another stay at that impressive venue, or even go one better and win automatic promotion.

The first problem to solve was the situation with his goalkeeper. Alan Marriott had been outstanding and, as an ever-present, had conceded only thirty seven goals in forty six games. He was out of contract and had other clubs pursuing him, but a combination of Keith's persuasion and the team spirit within the camp meant that Mazza was more than happy to sign on the dotted line and commit himself to Team Lincoln for another couple of years.

"My agent said that a couple of clubs watched me in the play-off games against Scunthorpe. Bradford City were one,

I think," he revealed. "I talked about it with my family. I realised that I loved Lincoln, the club and the place, and Keith was a great manager to work for. It had been good at Lincoln after being messed around at Spurs. Keith put the fun into football and you couldn't put a value on that."

Another area that needed addressing was at the other end of the pitch and Keith knew his side had to score more goals than they managed the season before. Never one to be swayed by the opinions of others, he ignored the jibes that his prime target had been voted Orient's worst ever player. As it was, he was pleased to be reunited with Gary Fletcher, who had played under him at Northwich, although he was as bemused as the rest of us when the player adopted a modern trend by taking on part of his new bride's name after their wedding and became Gary Taylor-Fletcher.

"Tommy Taylor was the manager at Orient and he'd picked me for all our eight friendly matches," said Fletcher. "I'd scored twelve goals in those games. Then he resigned. The decision was 'mutual' the club said. Paul Brush, the former youth team coach, took over. He didn't like lads like me who the club had paid a fee for and wanted to use his youth squad lads. Then he signed another striker just before the first match of the season so, despite me getting all those goals, I was dropped from the team. Then Keith rang. He was a good friend and he didn't get straight down to business. We chatted about our families and mutual friends. I went to watch Lincoln and then signed for them. Mark Bailey, who I knew from my Northwich days, was there, which helped too, but I was delighted to be back playing for Keith."

Away from the usual managerial duties of signing players and preparing the squad for the new season, Keith had an altogether more unsavoury matter to deal with. Alan Buckley had recruited his son, Adam, who had played a few games under his father's leadership. Keith, however, wasn't over-impressed with him as a player but he remained under contract and in the squad. Then news broke that Adam had been arrested over allegations of theft of items from the ground. The following month, Adam was sentenced to 120 hours of community service after pleading guilty to four counts of theft from his team-mates. Keith, of course, showed him the door, but it was a thoroughly unpleasant episode and a difficult one for Keith to deal with – bearing in mind his long relationship with Buckley's dad.

The players were instructed to return for pre-season training at the beginning of July and they would be checked to make sure they'd kept themselves fit and hadn't put on weight. Fines would be levied on those who had let things go a little bit. Keith's pre-season itinerary leading up to the first league match in early August was well constructed and comprised a mixture of training at the club, friendly matches against local clubs and a tour of Northern Ireland. After a full week of running and general fitness the squad, including the scholars, would play matches throughout the rest of July against Boston Town, Lincoln United, Bourne Town, Brigg Town, Frickley Athletic, Lincoln Moorlands and Gainsborough Trinity. Using his old contacts, Keith also arranged a game against Grimsby Town behind closed doors.

To introduce an element of fun in amongst all the hard work, he arranged for the squad to play golf after two or three of the training sessions. The tour across the Irish Sea took place over five days and inevitably included a match against his friends at Cliftonville. Keith's policy for trips away involved his players training, playing local opposition and having a darn good time. He knew that lads who got on socially would get on in matches, so a few beers and a few laughs were positively encouraged. At Gainsborough, Keith's team was made up of a few first team candidates and youngsters, and he sat high up at the back of the main stand, next to Radio Lincolnshire reporter Michael Hortin, to get a better view of the action. Like a lot of old stands, the seats in there are so close together that anyone over 5'6" ran the risk of having the blood supply cut off to their lower legs. Keith couldn't physically sit down unless he draped his long legs over the seat in front, which he did. Halfway through the first half, a steward approached and, presumably unaware he was talking to the Lincoln manager, barked to him that he should sit properly or get out. He may have been technically correct in what he said, but his manner was far from ideal.

"Keith just smiled, got up, left the stand and joined Gary on the touchline," said Hortin. "The guy was so rude but Keith didn't say a word. It was another little incident that showed me how cool Keith was in the way he dealt with things."

Pre-season is always a busy time for a club secretary, too, and Fran Martin would be busy registering players and filling in the small print of their contracts. She had worked for a couple of previous managers but found Keith the best so far.

"He was perfect to work for because from the day he started he established what his role was and then left me to get on with the things I was responsible for," she confirmed. "Some managers haven't got a clue about loans or seven-day approaches, that sort of thing, but Keith was spot-on. He was laid back and polite, even when we were under pressure to sign a player by a certain deadline. The only thing that let him down, as far as I was concerned, was his terrible sense of direction. So many times he'd head for a match to watch a player and then ring me from his car when he'd got lost. He'd put the phone on loudspeaker, say what road he was on, and then I'd look up where he was on the internet and guide him from street to street until he could see the floodlights. I'd be in fits of laughter by the time he eventually got there. And Keith was too, usually."

When it came to their role in running the club, the board were approaching the new season looking to do things very much as they did last time round. There are a lot of disparate activities at a football club – pro-football, commerce, corporate use, community work, lotteries; that sort of thing, and they all require efficient systems and a lot of hard work. But the board's overall policy was quite simple. Our role was to raise as much money as we could in every way possible, to keep costs down to a bare minimum and to make sure every penny was spent wisely. These simple but vital demands were not just our choice; they were the constraints we were still under having been through the administration process. There was one significant difference, though. One year ago the aim was to keep the club afloat and football was almost secondary.

This time we knew that Keith would still be operating with a small budget and we wanted to reward him by making that bit extra and boosting the coffers every way we could. He deserved it. We tried everything to bring in money and if it worked we would pass it on to him – even if the sums were often quite small. For example, if we could improve a sponsorship deal by £1,000 then, knowing how Keith worked, that might mean he'd be able to get a decent lad on loan for a month. Even the smallest expenses were ground down, sometimes cheekily, so that the saving could benefit the team. On away trips, director Keith Roe and I invariably travelled on the team bus. Pre-match meals were booked at a local hotel in advance by Fran Martin and she got some amazingly cheap deals.

We'd have to pay in cash because they knew we'd been in trouble and wouldn't accept a cheque from us. Quite often the number of Lincoln City staff who'd eaten the usual fare of boiled chicken and beans varied from the amount booked in advance because of injuries or players making their own way to the match, and we always made out the hotel had charged for too many. It became a challenge between Keith Roe and I each away trip to convince the reception staff that far fewer had dined in the restaurant than actually had, so that we paid the bare minimum. We took it in turns to see who could get the most freebies. At Bury I honestly believe we got about fifteen free meals.

The team bus is traditionally the manager's domain. It is 'an extension of the dressing room' as many managers will tell you. Despite this, Keith had no objection to our 'Director for a Day' idea, where up to two fans could make a healthy donation to our playing budget and then travel with the team and enjoy the away club's hospitality. Far from viewing it as a problem, Keith would welcome the guests, chat with them and make them feel part of the whole experience. Then, needless to say, one guy asked if his wife could come along and the question of a female entering this normally all-male enclave had to be broached. Keith had no problem with it and she was welcomed aboard. On a long trip to the south west, we even had a father and young daughter accompanying us as 'directors'. We won the match and the noise from the back of the coach was, for the first couple hours of the journey home at least, rowdy and boisterous. The language was colourful, to put it mildly. Then a player put on a DVD and we all had to watch the loudest goriest film in cinematic history. It was called something like *Death Blood Kill Shag*. If it wasn't, it should have been. In the early hours back at Lincoln as we all climbed out of the bus, I tentatively asked our guest if his teenage daughter had been OK with the things that had gone on. He smiled and said he'd been worried too until she casually told him to stop wittering and that she heard far worse at school every day of the week.

The board were well aware that their manager had done a tremendous job but was still on a low salary. Money was still very tight but we kept looking at ways we could improve things for him and Gary. The football world seems to hold few secrets and managers somehow know to the penny what counterparts at numerous rival clubs are earning and what their pro-football budget is. It therefore annoys the ones who are on less money but are doing a better job. It might not have been much but, as part of my day job running a very small architectural business, I was delighted to offer our services to measure up Keith's house and draw up plans for some alterations for him. We recommended some builders and soon his kids had a nice new playroom. It was nothing much, and it seems silly to relate it, but it was a little indication of how all of us wanted to help the guy as he worked away turning around the fortunes of our club.

It might have been a hangover from the season before but, despite Keith and Gary Simpson cajoling and encouraging from the sidelines, the team started the season poorly and results in the first few weeks were not encouraging. Then, in October, they started to improve, the team climbed into the top seven and even an FA Cup run seemed like it might be on the cards when the Imps beat Brighton 3-1 in a pulsating first round tie on a cold November afternoon at Sincil Bank. A rearranged friendly took place the same month against Kevin Keegan's Manchester City. Months earlier, one of his scouts who lived near Lincoln, being aware of his local club's financial difficulties, had persuaded his boss to bring his Premier League team to Sincil Bank for a pre-season friendly. This was a fantastic opportunity for our club. It was hoped that the game would be played during the previous close season and talks with officials at Manchester City were well underway. One morning around that time, I was a passenger in a fellow director's car travelling, ironically, to Maine Road for a Football League meeting. I used the time to make some calls including a long conversation with Keith about pro-football matters. Then someone rang me.

"Hello Rob, it's Kevin here," a voice said. I thought it was the Kevin who was supposed to be tiling my bathroom and had seemingly disappeared off the face of the earth.

"Now then Kevin," I said. "What's going on?"

"I've been thinking about our friendly. This summer we're going to have loads of the lads out on international duty," said Kevin. "I know it isn't as good but what if we play you later on in the year, say November?"

Spluttering, I realised it was actually Kevin Keegan on the other end of the phone. I thanked him for all his efforts and confirmed that I was sure our manager would be happy to play such a prestige game in among our league fixtures because it would be great for our fans, our players and would bring us in some very welcome extra revenue. I then rang Keith again and, as expected, he was fine about playing a friendly, even though the season would be well underway.

So it came to pass that Lincoln City entertained Manchester City in front of a near-capacity crowd. The occasion stimulated the Imps players to turn on some great stuff and only late goals from Paulo Wanchope and Nicolas Anelka enabled the visitors to come back from 2-0 down to earn a draw. After the game, Kevin Keegan stayed on the pitch for almost an hour signing autographs for our younger fans. I went over to thank him for everything he'd done. As I left him to the hordes of youngsters thrusting programmes in his direction, it occurred to me that, for all the pressures he was under, he was the sort of man who wanted to help a small club like ours. It seemed he'd got a personality very much like our own manager.

That wonderful friendly, the team getting results and the gradual financial recovery was leading us to think that things at Lincoln City were going well. Keith was happy, the fans were enjoying the new season and everything seemed fine.

*****

Then early one morning I got a call from Fran, our club secretary.

"Hi Fran, this is an early one. Are you OK?" I asked.

"I'm OK, but I've got some bad news," she said.

"What – Boston didn't win last night did they?" I joked, but then, from the tone at the other end of the phone, immediately realised that she meant something really bad.

She told me Keith had collapsed at home and had been rushed into Lincoln County Hospital. Although she didn't know what was wrong, she knew it was serious. I left the house and drove there as quickly as I could. I was shown to a side room in Accident and Emergency. Helen stood there in tears as Keith lay on a trolley, his eyes closed, and his arms and legs thrashing around. I was shocked and upset, but my uppermost thought was that I was an intruder at such an emotionally devastating time for his wife and family. Muttering something feeble about the club doing everything it could for him, I hugged Helen and left her with her husband and the staff who were busying themselves with what they had to do.

The next few hours and days were a horrendous mix of trying to do the right thing while not knowing what was going to happen to Keith. We were told he underwent brain scans and he had then been rapidly transferred to the Royal Hallamshire Hospital in Sheffield. Fran and I made sure the right people knew Keith was seriously ill and we deflected some of the more penetrating media questions. Although it seemed unimportant in terms of mere football, the board quickly agreed that Gary and Keith Oakes should take over running the team temporarily, if only to make sure the players had leadership to guide them through what was an awful time for all concerned.

It was then confirmed that Keith had suffered a double cerebral aneurism and he was to spend over eleven hours in the operating theatre in Sheffield. All this time we didn't know if he would survive and if he did, whether he would be permanently debilitated. I was desperate to know if his work for the club had led to this and if he'd been driving himself too hard. It seemed crazy because the words 'Keith Alexander' and 'laid back' always seemed to go together, but there he was, in intensive care on his forty-fifth birthday, and things like this weren't supposed to happen. It turned out he'd been at the ground in the morning, he and Gary had taken the reserves to their game at Mansfield in the afternoon and then he had watched Nottingham Forest reserves in the evening while Gary had gone to a game at Halifax. The general consensus was that this was just a normal day for a manager, especially ours, and his illness was the type that just happened if you were unlucky enough to draw the shortest of straws.

Best friend John Cockerill dashed to the hospital from North Lincolnshire. He sat with Helen until they told her Keith was being taken down to the operating theatre.

"Helen was too upset to go with Keith. I told her I'd go with him," said Cockerill. "I saw him lying there and didn't think he'd got a chance of coming through it. I asked the surgeon what his chances were. He said he'd do his best."

A spokesman for the Royal Hallamshire confirmed that "the operation went well but it is impossible to say what the outcome will be or how long Keith's recovery might take". This at least led us to tentatively breathe a collective sigh of relief because the word 'recovery' was being used. The atmosphere on the team bus as we travelled to Darlington a couple of days later was eerie because the manager wasn't there and playing football was an almost frivolously unnecessary thing to do.

"Straight after the gaffer was taken into hospital we were called into a team meeting," said Simon Yeo. "Gary came in and he was in tears. He told us we should prepare for the worst. The only thing we could do was do our best for Keith. It was difficult but that's what we did."

So their whole mindset was based on getting a result for their gaffer. Though their performance lacked its customary spark, they battled away and earned a creditable draw, backed by a huge away following who chanted Keith's name from start to finish. A week later, Lincoln played at home for the first time since his collapse. A big crowd witnessed an emotional occasion and poor Bristol Rovers didn't know what hit them as goals from Ben Futcher, Simon Yeo and Gary Taylor-Fletcher sealed a 3-1 win. The players wore T-shirts with photos of Keith on the front when they warmed up and, as Simon celebrated after his goal, he took off his home shirt to reveal the message 'Get well soon gaffer' underneath. Everyone knew that time, good luck and the best medical attention going was needed if the guy was to recover, but if goals, points and a passionate crowd helped, even in a tiny way, then they would be served up in abundance by the players and people involved with Lincoln City.

Whilst it wasn't common knowledge, season ticket holders and young fans would quite often answer their phones on their birthdays and be surprised to hear the manager of their club wishing them many happy returns. In September, former vice-chairman and elder statesman of Lincoln City, Jim Hicks, sadly passed away and Keith rang Jim's wife, Shirley, to offer his condolences. He made sure every member of his playing squad and background staff attended the funeral. These gestures, along with the hundreds of other generous acts Keith carried out without ever being prompted, probably explained why he received over 1,000 cards when it was him who was to experience his hour of need. They came from every corner of the football world, including fans, players, scouts, coaches, club officials, the football authorities and fellow managers, including Manchester United's Sir Alex Ferguson. It turned out Keith had only met Sir Alex once, at a sportsman's dinner years ago, but he was one of many who was willing our manager to recover. One evening, Fran and I went over to Sheffield to deliver another box of letters and cards and we were pleased to meet several members of Keith's family while we were there.

Eleven days after his operation, he was out of intensive care and conscious. The staff were quietly pleased about his progress.

"When he was in intensive care, Keith couldn't speak," explained Helen. "He didn't know what day or month it was, where he was or who was prime minister. He couldn't remember anything from everyday life. Then a nurse asked him about football and he wrote down all the clubs he played for, non-league and league, all in the right order. I was amazed."

Four weeks after his collapse and his operation, Keith was transferred back to Lincoln County Hospital. As his recovery continued, albeit he had a very long way to go, some of the old characteristics started to return, including his rebellious streak and the importance of football in his life.

"He was a nightmare as a patient," said Helen. "A nurse had to keep guard on his door because he'd keep getting up to try to leave the room."

"His illness shocked me to the core," said eldest son Matt. "I had a great job working away, but I gave it all up to move back to Lincoln to be near my dad. But Helen was right, he was a terrible patient. On one occasion the nurses dashed into his room because his heart monitor had flat-lined. They thought something terrible had happened. It turned out he'd taken the plug out to plug in his telly, so that he could get the football scores on Ceefax."

Whilst lots of people wanted to visit Keith, only family and close friends were allowed to do so. John Cockerill came over to see him as often as he could and was shocked at how poor Keith's memory was. During one visit, he was also surprised to see his pal get out of bed and leave the room, saying he was going to the toilet. Unaware that the patient was confined to the room, Cockerill patiently waited five minutes, then ten, until he got worried and called the nurse. She scolded him for letting Keith out and they dashed out in search of him. They eventually found him happily wandering along a corridor miles away chatting to people, oblivious to the panic he'd caused.

Back at the club, Gary, Keith Oakes and the players continued their boss's good work by picking up points regularly and maintaining their position near the top of the league. Their desire to 'do it for the gaffer' never wavered, especially when each report of his progress led everyone to be guardedly optimistic that he might one day return. At every home game, the club held collections for Neurocare, the charity raising funds for head injury patients at the Royal Hallamshire Hospital.

Finally, on 9th December, Keith was allowed home. His memory was poor, yet bizarrely, he could recollect a lot about football.

"He couldn't remember anything about our house. I had to keep showing him where our bedroom was," said Helen. "Several times he asked why he'd stayed in that hotel for such a long time. He couldn't even remember it was a hospital. I had to make sure I'd hidden the car keys. He wanted to drive to the ground and he was far from being allowed out, let alone able to drive."

Clearly Keith was delighted to be back with his family, but even they had to admit that it was work, as well as being with them, that drove him on.

"He was desperate to get back to the club. I never had a doubt he'd do it," said Matt.

After Christmas, it was rumoured Keith went to watch a couple of non-league games. It wasn't clear if this was with or without his doctor's blessing, but go he did. All the time, speculation mounted among Lincoln City supporters about him returning to resume his manager's role. We quite often had to remind them how ill he'd been and how it wouldn't happen for a while or, heaven forbid, at all if he didn't get the all-clear from his consultants.

In early New Year, I went along with a friend to the Scarborough versus Southend FA Cup replay. He was reporting on the game for a radio station and, as the winners would be at home to Chelsea in the next round, I thought it would be a cracking match to watch. On the way in we bumped into Neil Warnock, the then Sheffield United manager, who was there to summarise as part of the local radio coverage of the match. I was introduced to him and my role at Lincoln City was mentioned.

"Well, all I can say is well done," said Warnock. "A lot of clubs wouldn't do what you're doing."

I asked him what he meant and he said he'd heard, quite rightly, that our board were dotting the I's and crossing the T's on a new contract for our manager. All I could think of saying to him was "Well, you look after your own, don't you?" to underline our wish that Keith would fully recover and, having done so, would remain with us as long as possible. During the game I reflected that Warnock was right and, in the harsh world of football, maybe some clubs might not have been so keen to invest so readily in their manager for another couple of years if his health was in doubt. But such was the spirit at Lincoln, and so 'together' was our club through first financial troubles and then the physical adversity of our manager, that this really wasn't an option.

The speculation and rumour about Keith's state of health and his recovery continued. As a board we were content for him to take as long as he needed or, more especially, as long as his doctor instructed him to take, bearing in mind there had been the odd occasion when such advice hadn't quite been adhered to. Gary was doing a great job, even to the point of delivering excellent reports at board meetings, and the team were getting results. We were keen that Keith didn't publicly attend any of our games for his own sake but, knowing that he was desperate to watch the lads perform, we weren't too concerned about rumours that he might be slipping into the ground after a game had started to watch safely from a sponsor's private executive box.

At the start of the year, the weather was particularly bad and there were some severe frosts. One bitter Saturday afternoon, despite all the ground staff's best efforts, a home game was postponed very late on and a lot of fans were already at the ground. As a board we insisted on working hard all week but we had an unwritten rule that, after two o'clock on a match-day, work ceased. True to form therefore, as soon as we heard the match wasn't going to take place we adjourned to the bar that served the executive box holders. It seemed most people still at the ground had had the same idea so it was standing room only. Bearing in mind almost everyone in there hadn't seen Keith Alexander since he'd collapsed, didn't know his current state of health and certainly didn't have an inkling he was secretly attending the game, it was, on reflection, no surprise that when he walked in with his father the whole place fell hushed to an almost eerie silence. It was as if the almost impossible had happened, bearing in mind the seriousness of what had taken place all those weeks ago, such was the atmosphere. Then people started to talk again and the volume grew as people expressed their shock and delight at his arrival. Whilst not wanting to engulf him, most people wished Keith all the best. They clearly realised that a horribly cold winter afternoon and the disappointment that the game was off had paled into insignificance when they'd seen something that might signal the beginning of the end of a very trying period in the club's recent history.

"It makes you think. One minute you're here," said Keith, to a local reporter. "And the next minute, you're not." He sat with us in the directors box at our next match at Doncaster and enjoyed it, like we all did, when Lincoln won 2-0 against Rovers, who would have gone top had they beaten us. Before the game it was announced over the public address system that Keith was there and the whole crowd applauded, much to his embarrassment. Then, the following week in February, the recovery of the man, and the club in some ways, reached another milestone when Keith walked between a guard of honour formed by both teams and took his place in front of the home dug-out for the derby against Boston United, watched and applauded by a huge crowd.

After the game, Neil Thompson, the Boston manager, said he'd been pleased to welcome Keith back and have a quiet word as they stood waiting in the tunnel just prior to him walking out to the noise and emotion of the crowd.

"I must admit I asked him why the hell was he back so soon," said Thompson. "I said he should have more time off. He told me he needed to get back. 'If I have too long off, people won't want me,' he said."

It seemed strange that Keith would say that. He must have known how everyone wanted him fit and well first, and back working was well down the list of priorities. He knew we were keen to give him a new contract, whether his illness had changed him or not. It was the right thing to do. Clearly, Keith felt insecure at times, because of his experiences the first time at Lincoln and because of what happens to managers in the industry almost every day. But maybe he thought his desire to work harder than everyone else had set some sort of precedent and it was expected of him no matter what. I like to think we said things over the next days and months that reassured him.

Everyone has anecdotes about how Keith dealt with life back at the club after that. The supporters trust at Lincoln City has a gold members section for those who want to invest a bit more into the Imps than the rank and file members. At three home games each season they meet the board and then the manager before the match as part of the benefits they receive for their generous subscription. Geoffrey Piper, a Lincoln City supporter for more than fifty years, recalls the first such meeting after Keith's illness.

"Someone asked him if his brain was still OK for managing the football club," said Geoffrey. "After such a rather blunt question, Keith thought solemnly for a minute or so and then told us that he might have lost about half his brain but fortunately it was the part for doing things around the house and not the football part, so we should be alright."

Gary Simpson was pleased with his contribution during Keith's absence, but he was delighted to be back as second-in-command. Over the next few weeks he noticed that his gaffer had changed a little bit.

"The big guy has made a marvellous recovery, but he doesn't suffer fools as much. He's not as patient either," he revealed. "He's not happy that he isn't allowed to join in with training games, too, but he still keeps himself fit. Maybe it's no bad thing if he loses his temper more; he's been through the mill and he shouldn't have to put up with rubbish. He needs to think about himself a bit more now."

There wasn't anyone at Lincoln City who disagreed with that last sentiment.

9

Play-offs Again, Peterborough Problems

"It was fantastic being a City fan around that time"
Karl Mercer

Keith soon slipped back into manager mode, especially when it came to signing players. He had an eye for good lads who might have lost their way and who, if signed up, might join the club on a wage his budget would allow. Jamie McCombe was one of these. He had fallen out with his manager at Scunthorpe, was out of the team and was, in fact, banished to training either on his own or with the youth squad. He fitted the bill perfectly for Keith, being a giant centre-half who could push up and nick a goal if necessary. The deal was done, then it was blocked and a few weeks later in February it was allowed to go through by a Football League tribunal. Jamie slotted in alongside Ben Futcher, another tall lad to put it mildly, and the push for promotion continued.

Another former waif and stray, Gary Taylor-Fletcher, was repaying his new boss's faith in him by scoring at regular intervals. His moment of personal justice came in March when he scored both goals in a 2-0 win at former club Orient, one of which followed an amazing dribble through the heart of their defence. He was applauded off by both sets of fans when Keith, anticipating it would get a good reaction, substituted him with a few minutes to go. The player had certainly got a fair bit of respect back after the home club's jovial comments about his ability during his time there.

The season ended when the 'Huddersfield jinx' struck again. The very name ended up striking dread into every Lincoln fan's heart. First, there was the tremendous 3-1 home win over them which was overshadowed by club president John Jennison having a heart attack in the stand as the final whistle blew. I stood with his son, Charles, watching helplessly as my wife, Polly, a nurse, and the medical team pounded on his chest and brought him back to life. Later in hospital they confirmed he'd 'died' three times but he went on to make a full recovery. Then, in the return fixture in March, Pavel Abbott scored the winner for the home side in the most bizarre fashion after being at least twenty yards offside. It had to be seen to be believed and the referee broke the world sprint record when he blew the final whistle and headed for the tunnel to avoid the grilling he was going to get from Keith, Gary, the players and everyone else connected with Lincoln City.

Finally, after we'd lost narrowly at home in the play-off semifinal first leg to the Yorkshire club, we found ourselves 2-0 up at half-time at their place. It could have been 5-0 such were the chances we missed. In the second half another refereeing triumph did for us when, after an hour, Andy Booth fell over in our area with a full yard between him and defender Jamie McCombe. Despite our protests the penalty was given and then converted. They equalised seven minutes from time and the game ended 2-2, with Huddersfield's first-leg advantage taking them to the final.

Keith didn't miss out on a trip to Cardiff, however, although being a pundit as part of Sky's coverage of the play-off final between Huddersfield and Mansfield Town wasn't exactly what he had in mind. Lincoln fan Karl Mercer was another intruder there, having agreed to drive his uncle and two nephews, each one a Stags fan, to the game. Keith had got to know Karl after he went to support the Imps on a pre-season tour in France.

"What the heck are you doing here?" asked Keith, making

his way to his seat nearby.

As if to confirm he hadn't changed allegiances, Karl unzipped his jacket to reveal a Lincoln City badge on his shirt and explained he'd got roped into a chauffeuring job.

"He laughed and told me to enjoy the game," said Karl. "He often had a word with me, at supporters meetings, when I collected a ticket at the ground and bumped into him, times like that. He always found time to have a chat. I'll never forget how together Keith, Gary and the squad were when we saw them training in France. They worked hard but had fun. It was fantastic being a City fan around that time."

A couple of weeks later I had a meeting with Keith just before he went off on holiday. He surprised me by asking if the board thought he'd failed by not getting us promoted. Bearing in mind his illness, reaching the play-offs, a much improved average gate, more debt paid off, the fans all being happy and the club having a better squad of players from the year before, with some of them worth a fair bit now, I was able to reassure him that we wouldn't be rushing to replace him just yet. I think Keith got the message.

*****

"I really can't believe some Lincoln City fans want manager Keith Alexander sacked." So began the 'Froggy's Focus' column in the *Lincolnshire Echo* in early September 2004. The article, penned by Lincoln-born former England player Steve Froggatt, continued: "They must be absolutely stupid. You only have to take a look at what he has achieved in the last couple of seasons. OK, the Imps have made a dodgy start, but a manager should only be judged on where his side are at the end of a season."

Despite Gary Taylor-Fletcher equalling a long-standing club record by scoring in all of Lincoln's first six games, the club found themselves sitting in twentieth position after a quarter of the new season. A small minority of disgruntled fans were making their views known, but the vast majority felt that this was a false position and they trusted their manager and his squad to turn it around.

In October, Keith and I represented the club at the Brian Clough memorial service at Pride Park in Derby. I had a doctor's appointment late on so we arranged for Keith to pick me up from the surgery and drive us both there. I had a mole on my back that was becoming irritating and the doctor quickly confirmed that it was nothing particularly significant. He added that, if I liked, he could get the nurse to whip it off there and then. 'Like' wasn't a word I would have chosen, but to avoid having to come back, I agreed. I then waited what seemed an eternity for the nurse to call me in, inject some anaesthetic, cut off the unsightly lump and put in a couple of stitches. All the time I knew it was getting later and later and Keith would be waiting in his car outside. By the time I jumped into the passenger seat, flustered and mumbling apologies, it was far too late to get to the service on time.

Keith couldn't have been more patient and didn't seem concerned at all about our late arrival, even though I knew he would hate to appear disrespectful by rolling up after the start of such an important football occasion. When we got there we found seats and listened to the tributes and hymns, or tried to. We must have been in the only part of the ground where the PA system was worse than the one at Sincil Bank. Every spoken word or musical note sounded the same – crackling and incomprehensible. Thankfully, the service was interrupted by a brief interval and my guilt at getting our manager there late was relieved a little by us moving around and finding seats where we could see and hear everything clearly. Keith pointed out a great many people and many of them greeted him warmly.

The ceremony restarted and we listened with increasing incredulity as Geoffrey Boycott, the former Yorkshire and England cricketer, stood on the podium, obviously tasked to pay tribute to the great man, and proceeded to speak at great length and in great detail about himself. I glanced round to where some of the Nottingham Forest stars of old were sitting and saw that they were hardly able to contain their laughter. Old Big 'Ead, as Brian Clough was known, may have sadly passed away, but there were obviously others still around who also had a fairly high opinion of themselves. After the service, we went into a function room and Keith was soon chatting away with one football person or another. I was amazed at the number of people he knew and the number of people who came up to him. Thankfully, I found a couple of Lincoln fans to latch on to who knew the Clough family. On the journey home we chatted all the way and Keith spoke about some of the people at the service and how they were often different from how the public perceived them. He told me that Aston Villa's Martin O'Neill was a great manager and was excellent at communicating to his players, but in everyday life he was quite a shy and nervous guy.

Also that month Keith and Helen flew to Belfast to attend the Cliftonville 125th anniversary banquet. Supporter Liam Murray volunteered to collect them from the airport and was delighted to chat with them on the short journey.

"Keith spoke with great affection about our club," he recalled. "He said he hadn't known what to expect when he first signed but he was overwhelmed by how everyone at the club had taken him to their hearts. All three of us agreed he should have signed for us much sooner than he did! He got another rousing reception in the City Hall as they both entered."

Back on the playing front, new signing Gareth McAuley, another astute acquisition, this time through Keith's contacts in Northern Ireland, started to make an impact. During a conversation with best friend John Cockerill, Keith asked him to come to a Lincoln home game and run the rule over his new centre-half. "He'll do you a job, no problem" was Cockerill's brief but encouraging assessment. McCauley helped tighten up the defence and the side started to win more games than they lost.

The home form had been poor but that started to pick up too. Keith had made changes to try to improve the performances at Sincil Bank and he'd even adopted an idea brought up in the boardroom. As a chairman I was a bit of a wimp when it came to communicating to the players. I was OK at chairing board meetings and doing the PR stuff but, for some reason, I never really felt at ease mixing with the guys who did the business on the pitch. I once had to address them all as they sat in the dressing room after training and explain how their new bonus system worked which, on reflection, was fair, reasonably generous but far too complicated. Keith had asked me to put it direct to them because I don't think he understood it either. Or maybe he thought that if the board were going to come up with such a complicated scheme then they could damn well explain it themselves. I stood there waffling on, gradually sensing that, to a man, they were probably thinking 'Who is this pillock and what on earth is he on about?'

However, my one 'dynamic' idea in terms of the playing side occurred around this time. Our away form was good but, as I mentioned, we couldn't win at home. I suggested to Keith that we treat a home fixture like an away one and travel out of Lincoln and back again on the team bus. Keith agreed that it was worth trying, probably to be polite and humour me rather than genuinely thinking it was some sort of masterstroke. It showed, however, that he might have his ways of operating but he was always open to suggestions from others. For once I felt like a 'proper' chairman who had so much money and so much power that everyone did what he said. As if.

So it was that, prior to our home match against Northampton Town, the Lincoln City squad headed off to a hotel at Belton Woods, near Grantham, for a very brief stay before travelling back again and disembarking from the coach in front of the home dressing room. I watched the players as they stepped out of the bus and their faces bore the expressions of a group of people wondering what the hell they had just done all that for.

The match got underway and we were 2-0 down at half-time. Then, miracle of miracles, everything clicked and the fightback began. A late goal secured a 3-2 win and we were all delighted. After the game, already knowing that the 'away-day' idea had probably had little connection with the turn of events on the pitch, I asked Keith if the trip on the team coach had helped, smiling broadly as if to let him know I knew it hadn't. As kind and respectful as ever, he said that it might have contributed, but the "the biggest fucking bollocking they've ever had" at half-time might have helped too.

By December, things were looking much better and we had climbed up to fifth place in League Two. Whilst those now silent, unhappy supporters had urged the manager to change his methods, it was his insistence on sticking to his principles, apart from the odd departure to appease his chairman, that had got the team winning again.

"He hardly ever ranted or raved, to be fair. It was an exception when he did," said goalkeeper Alan Marriott. "If the team had played badly or just one or two individuals had struggled, he was always the same. He had faith in us. His team talk just before kick-off was just about the same every game. He'd point towards the opposition dressing room and say 'I wouldn't swap any of you fuckers with any of them in there'."

And, unlike a lot of other managers, he wouldn't lay into some of the less confident players. "People like Peter Gain and me weren't as strong characters as some of the others," said Marriott. "If we made a cock-up, we'd go into a shell. The gaffer knew this and he'd tell us to forget our mistake and remember all the good things we were capable of."

The players also began to feel more affection for their manager and his ways the longer they played for him and the more they knew him.

"He was a character, the gaffer," said the goalkeeper. "We were on an away trip once; one where we travelled on a Friday and stayed overnight in a hotel near the away club's ground. During our evening meal we were all there, the players and the backroom staff, in our club tracksuits. Keith had his yellow socks on too, as always. We started to notice that, while he was eating, he was eyeing up all the waiters, looking them up and down, and we hadn't a clue what he was up to. Then one of them, a really lanky guy, pulled up a chair near the gaffer and he swapped his black shoes for Keith's size twelve trainers. He carried on serving us, wearing the gaffer's training shoes. It turned out that Keith had forgotten to pack his ordinary clothes and he needed some normal shoes for when he, Gary and Keith Oakes got changed and went out for a drink later on. As it was, he went out into town wearing a borrowed white dress shirt, track-suit bottoms and a hotel waiter's black shoes."

As the season reached its climax, Lincoln were again looking like candidates for automatic promotion and, if not, then at least another shot at the play-offs was on the cards. Simon Yeo was back in the team and was on his way to notching over twenty league goals, closely followed by Gary Taylor-Fletcher on the leading scorer chart. Keith was looking well, the attendances were even higher than the season before and everything in the garden seemed rosy. Anyone who has been involved in a football club will tell you that it is never plain sailing, however well things seem to be going on the pitch. But whether it was a glitch in the club finances, players' personal problems, fall-outs between people at the club or one of any number of other problems large or small, Keith, the staff or the board would deal with it.

For example, we had an occasion when two players fell out big-style after a team night out. One of them, a black striker, snapped when the bad feeling continued as they met up for training a couple of days later. Claiming he'd been racially abused, he thumped the other player good and proper. In fact the guy on the receiving end was projected on to the bonnet of Gary Simpson's car and the large dent left in it helped to confirm pretty clearly what had gone on. Keith reported the incident to me, he described what he intended to do, both players were disciplined with the punishment matching the seriousness of their misbehaviour and we moved on. Problem solved.

However, as we approached the end of the season, an issue arose that wasn't quite as straightforward to attend to. I had decided that I would be standing down as chairman at the end of the season and wrote to all the members of the board to confirm so. I explained that, as I was elected by the fans, I shouldn't hog the position and, after five years, it was time to let someone else have a go at being the trust's representative on the club board. I also needed to concentrate on my small business more, it having suffered a bit by my being at the club so much, week in week out. I'd also recognised that, whilst I wasn't a bad bloke to have banging the drum and getting people to help the club when it was financially wounded, Lincoln City FC needed some skilled leadership now that it was making profits and it could be capitalising on that in business terms.

Once the directors had been made aware that I was quitting, I was then going to tell the local press and radio. Except I couldn't. Just at the same time we were contacted by a season ticket holder whose job led him to travel around in the East Midlands. He explained that, as a mad keen fan, he was far from happy contacting us about something he'd seen, but felt he had no alternative. He went on to explain that he had stopped for lunch in the Fox and Hounds pub at Longthorpe, near Peterborough, and had seen Keith, a group of his players and Peterborough owner Barry Fry all enjoying lunch together. It didn't take a lot of working out what was going on and it was a very serious matter for the club to deal with. Also my standing down, albeit not particularly important, couldn't be announced when, at the same time, it appeared our manager and some of his players were looking at what another club could offer. We had to deal with it from a disciplinary point of view, let alone the problem of what we did as a club if they left us. As expected, some of our directors were outraged, but first we had to establish that our fan's information was genuine. I could see why the incident had upset board members, because they were successful businessmen and they would never tolerate their own contracted staff visiting competitors to look at opportunities elsewhere, especially in work-time paid by them.

Personally, I wasn't too bothered about that. Having been involved in football for a few years now, I knew that managers and players talked to other managers and players, and chairmen too, off the record, before any sort of open formal process kicked in. It was like the directors who'd say they preferred our players to be clean-living local lads. I'd say I didn't give a toss if they were chain-smoking, beer-swilling oafs with the carnal ambitions of a field full of rabbits as long as they never broke the law and got us near the top of the league. I was upset, however, that Keith and his lads were thinking of leaving Lincoln. They were doing us proud but, again, I was always aware this might happen and it was up to us as a club to make sure people we wanted to stay wanted to themselves.

At one of our weekly meetings I told Keith we'd been told he'd been seen with Barry Fry and he denied it. After describing his reaction to the board, I then met him again a couple of days later. During our chat about his budget, forthcoming fixtures and so on, I dropped into the conversation that we were taking action against the fan who had told us about his alleged meeting at Peterborough, because his comments had caused difficulties within the club. Next morning Keith rang and asked me to meet him.

"I did go to Peterborough, chairman," were his first words when we met up in the boardroom.

"I know you fucking did," were mine.

"Barry asked us to go," said Keith. "And I didn't see any harm in it. We wanted to look at the facilities there. We can't guarantee we'll be at Lincoln for the rest of our careers."

"I know how football works Keith," I said. "But you're under contract here. Your players are too. And we want you and them to stay."

"We will stay, chairman. We're happy here, especially if we can get promotion."

"That's fine," I replied. "But you can see why the directors are angry. And me too, to some extent. They are successful business people and, in their own companies, they don't take kindly to key staff swanning off to suss out new jobs. They want their staff to concentrate on working hard for them."

I told him I'd speak to the board and let him know the outcome. All I knew, thinking about the meeting afterwards, was that Keith had intended nothing malicious and his reaction said so. He genuinely didn't think a little trip to see what another club had to offer was something to worry about. As the meeting had proceeded, he had, however, become concerned that he'd upset some of the directors.

The board met and some people were still, quite understandably, far from happy. They thought Keith should be sacked, however much they would be saddened by such an outcome. Others felt, like me, that it was a regrettable turn of events but people in football do these things. Everyone was delighted with Keith as a person and what he'd done for the club and we were all enjoying being near the top of League Two again. The view was also expressed that, as long as this sort of thing wasn't going to happen again, we'd work hard at keeping him with the club for as long as possible. Eventually, with no obvious consensus reached, we had to vote on the matter. Sod's law prevailed and with the votes tied, one of my last significant actions as chairman of the club was to use my casting vote.

"Do you want to change your vote to 'for' or 'against?'" I asked a director who had abstained. He didn't. 'Thanks a bunch' I thought.

"I appreciate your view that the manager has made a big

mistake," I said, directing my comments to the directors who felt that Keith should go. "It's a form of betrayal. But this industry is like no other. Clubs don't hesitate to sack managers after a bad run of results. So football people are always on the lookout. They never know what's around the corner. I understand that. And another reason I'm sticking with my vote for Keith to stay is because the club would suffer badly if he was sacked."

I cast my vote and Keith survived. One director, Ray Trew, was still unhappy and resigned that evening. Fortunately he was persuaded to withdraw his resignation a day later. Keith was told of our decision and, safe in the knowledge that we wouldn't be having to reveal our manager's departure, and safe from the quite understandable conspiracy theories that would have concluded that his going and mine were connected, I was able to tell the local media, at long last, that I'd be standing down after the final match of the season.

We didn't make it into one of the automatic promotion places, so we were to take our chances in the play-offs for the third season in a row. The latest budding star recruited by Keith, McCauley, scored the winner in the home play-off semifinal against Macclesfield and again at their place when we drew the second leg 1-1. We were back at the Millennium Stadium again.

"Late on, Keith changed his mind about staying at Celtic Manor," recalled Alan Marriott. "He didn't want us to think it was another great occasion like last time and take our minds off winning the final. We stayed at the Vale of Glamorgan Hotel, near Cardiff, instead. Mind you, he did joke we'd get another new suit to replace the one we got last time, so we'd at least have some more nice new clobber again."

Despite being the better side for an hour, Lincoln didn't take their chances. The one we did convert was ruled out, wrongly we thought, for offside. The Imps players tired and Southend seemed stronger as the match went into extra-time. Once they scored we knew it was all over and when they added a second it didn't seem to matter. Unlike last time at Cardiff, this was just another match in the pursuit of promotion and we were all bitterly disappointed. The only consoling factor was that we'd got a great squad and maybe next year we'd go all the way and go up automatically.

*****

As arranged, I stood down after the Southend game. As an ordinary fan, it had been an honour to have been chairman of the club I supported but it was time to let go. It had been an amazing experience but it had also been extremely hard work. There had been some astounding highs and some desperate lows. I'd got memories I'd cherish for the rest of my life and that I'd bore my kids and grandkids with for years to come.

One of the best parts of doing the job, if not the best part, was working with Keith. I'd worked with three managers in total and was the link between them and the board of directors. Phil Stant and Alan Buckley were both gentlemen, despite the difficult circumstances the club was in during their time at Sincil Bank. But my time with Keith was the longest and the most rewarding. From the off, I decided that it would be unwise to get too friendly with any manager. I've seen chairmen and directors who like to mix socially with them, whether it be out on the golf course, in restaurants or that sort of thing. They like to be seen with them. Few managers would refuse this, because they wouldn't wish to disappoint their superiors and possibly affect their working relationship. But there may, and probably will, be times when a chairman needs to stamp down on something, such as the way a budget is being used or, worse still, have to take drastic action if circumstances warrant it, and being friends would make that harder.

Despite this self-imposed restriction, I felt that Keith and I were close professionally, appreciated the difficulties we worked under and hit it off pretty well. He was always approachable and respectful, even when sometimes he didn't like what I had to tell him. And as the team kept managing to win more games than it lost, we had some enjoyable conversations about football, his squads and how he liked to play the game. Many times I wanted to give my opinion on a player or a tactic but clearly I couldn't do this. I was just a fan and it wouldn't be right. I sometimes phrased a question in a way that sounded like I was relaying what some fans thought, but he used to see through this, smile, and from his reply I knew I hadn't got a clue. We once went to a game to look at a team we were due to play soon after; about the only time I accompanied Keith on such a mission. I said I thought a midfield player, who used to play for us under a previous manager, was useful and I was surprised we'd let him go. In a few seconds, Keith put me straight by telling me the lad had no stamina, didn't have the legs to get from box to box and was a spent force after about an hour. The theory that the average fan hasn't got much idea what actually goes on during a match made sense to me when Keith had explained this and lots of other things.

We met regularly, either in the boardroom or in his office, to discuss pro-football matters. Inevitably, especially in his first season, the main priority was to go over his budget and make sure his spending was sticking within very strict limits. It meant getting value from every penny because money was tight. It always amazed me how Keith, with his own very peculiar accounting system, made his month-by-month figures tally with those prepared by the club accountant. One month, well into the season, I berated him, much to his surprise, for being so far out with his bottom-line figure, until I revealed he was just £4 over budget and I was well and truly joking. I knew my limitations when it came to the accounts. Other directors also had an input into how Keith spent his budget. Director Keith Roe was a master when it came to raising money, and even better at spending it to our best advantage, and he too was impressed by our manager's unconventional but skilful financial acumen.

From what I could see, a large part of what made Keith a good manager was his overall philosophy to the game and, wider than that, to life in general. He got worked up sometimes and he got angry, as a fair few referees could testify. But he never overdid it; he never went ballistic. He went so far and then his calm side would kick in and he'd be level-headed about things. After a home draw, when we'd been desperate to win, he'd reflect that we'd won the previous away game and we'd have settled for four points from the two games. And we'd stop wittering and realise he was right. Win, lose or draw, he'd always come up to the boardroom after a game to answer our questions, giving off the air of someone who'd make sure we'd keep a good run going or would get the team winning again. He never over-celebrated when we won and he never ranted when we lost. He just knew we'd do OK at the end of the season, whatever the result at the time. The old 'there or thereabouts' thing I suppose.

I enjoyed being chairman, even though it just about did my head in. The reason I liked it, despite the stress and the tension, was for the great wins, the magic atmosphere at a lot of the games, and the way the club, because of Keith, became a true 'club' in the literal sense of the word, with us all in it together. But the main reason I enjoyed it was because I got the chance to work with a good man who led us out of the wilderness and showed us anything was possible. I was lucky. I was an ordinary fan who got the chance to be chairman of his club. But I was doubly lucky because I did it while Keith Alexander was there as manager, and not many people are as lucky as that.

10

Gardening Leave, London Road, Gigg Lane

"Keith was upset that he was getting the push . . .
he was very, very disappointed"
Barry Fry

You can't beat it. A festive local derby, and you find yourself queuing up to get in the away end with a burger in one hand, a hot sweet tea in the other and your head still pounding after the excesses of the night before. Headache or no headache, like everyone around you, you have every expectation that the game is going to be a cracker. And so we found ourselves on a chilly New Year afternoon at Mansfield, and although the Imps were lying only around halfway in the table, we hoped a win at Field Mill would kick-start the second half of the season and we would have another crack at promotion. Then optimism and jokes turned to concern as rumours spread along the line of fans.

"Keith's not here. He's been suspended," said the guy behind us. Knowing I used to be on the board, a few people asked me if I knew what had happened. As I'd said numerous times since the close season when asked about new signings or other club gossip, I could only confirm that I wasn't involved anymore and I hadn't a clue what was going on. I hadn't spoken to Keith much since I'd stood down, but in this case the temptation was too great. If he wasn't at a game and it didn't involve something like an impending move to a bigger club, it could only be something unpleasant that had caused it, so I went to one side and rang him.

"You OK Keith? What's going on?" I asked.

"I don't know chairman, I only wish I knew," sighed Keith, still faithfully addressing me by the title I'd relinquished months ago.

"Have you been getting grief about the results?"

"No, no-one's said anything."

"Is it anything to do with the Peterborough business?" I asked.

"I don't think it's that either. I don't know what the problem is."

"Well I hope it gets sorted out," I said. "This is crazy."

"Thanks chairman, I'll keep in touch," said Keith.

As the teams came out at five to three, we noticed Gary wasn't there either and youth team coach John Schofield was the man shouting instructions from the touchline as Lincoln battled away in an appropriately disappointing game that ended goalless.

The next day, the club announced that Keith and Gary had been put on 'gardening leave'. No reasons were given, so we were left as bemused by it all as we were at Mansfield. The local paper, the *Lincolnshire Echo*, ran the headline 'Chaos at City' over an article that included the brief statement by the board of directors. Several other pages were devoted to speculation about reasons for the suspensions and possible successors if Keith was not to return. The paper also printed contributions from disgruntled fans who questioned the decision and demanded an explanation from the board. John Schofield was quoted, describing how the players had been told. In the close season the directors had decided to elect Steff Wright as chairman of the board and Ray Trew as chairman of football. He described how both of them had entered the away dressing room at Field Mill together and informed the players that their manager and his assistant were suspended.

"I just told the lads to go out on to the pitch before they got changed, to clear their heads," said Schofield. "I thought that was the best thing to do because it had certainly come as quite a shock to them."

The next few days featured hastily arranged board meetings and increasing speculation about the reasons for the board's actions. *The Echo* continued to be inundated with letters from angry fans who resented their manager being suspended and were unhappy about being kept in the dark. Keith's agent was quoted as saying his client was very upset and, even if the matters were resolved, Keith would find it very hard to work for the club and act as if everything had gone back to normal.

Helen Alexander was very unhappy too. "I was just about to go to work when Keith was told not to come to the club," she said. "I was too upset to go. I couldn't believe it, after all he'd done. The first time he got into a bit of trouble and he'd got the sack. He hadn't fully been sacked I suppose, but it certainly felt like it. It was the first time I felt insecure about him being a manager and how it could affect us."

Then, on Friday, 6th January, the club announced that Keith was back in charge. Their statement included a public apology for his suspension. It wasn't all sweetness and light, though, as reports confirmed that Gary Simpson had left the club and one of the joint chairmen, Ray Trew, who was in charge of football matters and had invested substantially into the club, had resigned.

The Echo didn't hold back when they gave their opinion of this latest turn of events. Their front page featured the letters LCFC in red down the left side, with each letter spelling out the words Lunacy, Chaos, Farce and Confusion. The front page article began "Lincoln City were today the laughing stock of the football world." Inside the paper, an editorial blasted the club with both barrels, saying:

"In 2002, Lincoln City were on the verge of financial extinction but, thanks to the fans, the crisis was averted. Four years on and a new danger is threatening City – a danger from people who say they have the club's best interests at heart. So when City's board members awake this morning, they should feel ashamed. Their handling of the past few days has been a shambles. Treating your fans with contempt is bad enough, but to nearly lose one of your most successful managers in twenty years is just madness. To then admit boss Keith Alexander did nothing to warrant being put on gardening leave is a joke no City fan will today find funny. The affair has been handled so badly even chairman of football Ray Trew has resigned. Trew offered hope to Lincoln City and had a genuine ambition to take the club forward, only for events in the boardroom to force him to quit. Perhaps the biggest sin of all is that the club is a laughing stock within football. It is now time for the people in charge to deliver answers to the fans – and quickly. Why was this complete PR disaster allowed to happen? What is the real reason behind Trew's exit? Who is in charge? The fans are being left in the dark and it is unacceptable. Today the *Echo* asks if this is how hard-working fans who helped the club to survive deserve to be treated. Please Lincoln City, that is a question we all want answering."

Leigh Curtis had arrived as a football reporter at the *Echo* relatively recently and he had quickly built up a friendship, albeit a professional one, with the manager, who would come to be the subject of many of his reports.

"Keith was very good at finding some common ground, so your conversation never faltered. He always sought out something about you so that you were comfortable with him," said Leigh. "Mind you, one of my early reports said that Lincoln's display had 'the ghost of Alan Buckley's tactics about it'. The next thing I know, Keith was on the phone saying that I'd better not write bollocks like that or I wouldn't last long. I would have been worried but he was laughing away when he said it and he then asked me when I was coming down to the ground for a cup of tea. Whenever I interviewed him we'd have tea and chocolate biscuits in his office. He'd never rush me to get it over with, and usually he'd ask if I wanted to stay around and watch the players train. He used to like his sayings. He'd say 'They've ruined my weekend so I'll ruin theirs' when the team had lost and he was thinking of getting them in for training instead of giving them the next day off. And whenever you greeted him and asked how he was, he'd always say 'Keeping my head above water, thanks'. I think 'You don't half write a load of bollocks' became another of his favourite sayings when he was talking about my match reports."

Leigh soon became aware of the methods Keith used.

"Keith's spell at Lincoln was very special. The camaraderie he developed was something else. There was no backbiting and he kept a sort of non-league spirit in the club, where players would be happy to train or play and then socialise all together and with the fans. Players would leave but he'd replace them with guys with the same attitude so the spirit in the squad was the same."

As a result, Leigh was as puzzled as everyone else about the events that had thrown the club into turmoil. Keith had returned from illness and continued to work wonders. For him to be removed from the club for reasons that never became clear seemed almost irrational.

Over the next couple of days, as Keith returned to Sincil Bank, the fall-out continued, with two more directors, Keith Roe and Kevin Cooke, leaving the club, although Cooke remained as company secretary.

It was never revealed exactly what had caused the board to suspend Keith and Gary. Clearly, the day trip to Peterborough the season before had made people extremely wary, and that was understandable. It was rumoured that misdemeanours within the pro-football part of the club, including an overspend in the budget and the lack of movement of players out to balance it, had brought all this up again, although there was little evidence of any massively serious wrong-doing. These misdemeanours had maybe started to irritate people who felt that Keith and his staff had to be squeaky clean after his reprieve last season. Trew was the director who had resigned over the Peterborough business, albeit he was quickly persuaded to withdraw his resignation, and he was bound to be keen that things were done by the book. Similarly, the board's decision to have a chairman of football and a chairman of the board hadn't helped, because it had led the board to be split into two distinct camps with damaging results. So much so that, as Keith and his squad started to put together yet another promotion push over the next few weeks, behind the scenes recriminations and talk of takeovers rumbled on. This animosity was something that would stay with the club for a very long time.

Ironically, as soon as Keith reported back to work and, despite the absence of his right-hand man, the team started to perform. They went on an impressive unbeaten run and, much to everyone's relief, reports of points won and good performances featured in the local press, rather than other more damaging issues. The squad battled away, the fans were enjoying it and it seemed like the good times had returned. Keith and his players had a togetherness similar to that of the last few seasons and people started to think this could be the year promotion would finally be won.

Whilst working tirelessly to gain success, Keith, as always, never forgot his roots. For the return game against Mansfield he invited the old Wembley-winning Stamford team to Sincil Bank. They always had an annual gathering and Keith would attend, but this time he arranged for them all to have tickets for the executive club and, after the game, joined them for drinks and a couple of hours of laughter and reminiscing.

Leigh Curtis, however, was concentrating on the present and was convinced the Lincoln team ethic would be the thing to help them achieve success.

"I'd see Keith every Friday so that we could write a good build-up to the Saturday game," he said "The spirit in the dressing rooms, judging by the noise after training, told me it could be their year. Mind you, they still wouldn't stand any funny business from anyone who was a bit 'above it', shall we say."

Maheta Molango had been signed on loan from Brighton to add a bit more fire power up front, but he'd only scored one goal and made as many appearances on the subs bench as he did in the starting eleven. Leigh sat in Keith's office one morning when suddenly Maheta burst in. He was obviously very worked up and Keith, as he offered Leigh another bourbon biscuit, calmly asked him what the problem was.

"The keys to my X3 have gone missing. Someone has stolen my car keys – again," he spluttered. "If I'd have wanted to be in a circus, I'd have bloody joined one!"

Keith sighed as he stood up and wandered over to his office door. He opened it and, with several of the players laughing and elbowing each other at the far end of the corridor, shouted: "Whichever one of you fuckers has got his keys, fucking give him 'em back now!"

He shepherded the annoyed player out of the office, sat back down at his desk, looked at Leigh and cracked out laughing.

"They are a bunch of fuckers, they really are," he said, barely concealing his affection for his lads and their antics.

One former Lincoln player, Grant Brown, was very upset at being released by Keith a couple of years earlier but later realised that he too was well thought of by his former boss. Brown had made a record 407 league appearances for the Imps but found himself without a contract when Keith took over from Alan Buckley as part of his cost-cutting measures. Brown signed for Telford but was allowed to train all week at Sincil Bank.

"Keith knew it was convenient for me to train with his lads to save me travelling a lot," said Brown. "Then he said he liked me being there because I didn't hold back in eleven versus eleven practice games. I was delighted when the gaffer asked me to come back to Lincoln this season as youth team coach. I learned a lot from watching Keith at training. He was very fair but he was also ruthless. Players who went too far soon knew it. He'd often fall out with Franny Green, for example, so he'd leave him out of the team to send out the right message to the others. Then he'd pick him again to show there were no hard feelings and to show the players that, whatever happens, if you keep working hard you can overcome the bad times."

Lincoln were unbeaten in their last six games of the season and gained a point in their last home game in front of a large crowd to guarantee their place in the play-offs for the fourth successive season. Results that afternoon meant that their opponents would be local rivals Grimsby Town, one of Keith's old clubs. Sadly, Lincoln played poorly in the first game, losing 1-0 at home and, despite a spirited performance at Blundell Park, lost there too, with one of Keith's old players, Ben Futcher, scoring for the hosts. Yet again the feeling of being so near yet so far was upon us and it was very disappointing to know that the club was destined for another season in the bottom division.

Keith had often surprised people by questioning his own achievements. He seemed to look at things differently because an outsider would usually say he'd done a great job. But he would always be watching out, if not for the knife in the back, then the jovial slap on the back that would be accompanied by the vote of confidence that was less than sincere and meant he was in trouble. He'd been very unhappy at the suspension episode and again he'd failed to get the club promoted from a promising position. So, even if most people in charge at the club thought it had been another good season, he had his doubts, both about what the powers that be might do and whether he himself could have done more.

*****

During the summer, Keith completed his UEFA Pro-Licence course. Always keen to continue his education, this signalled his arrival at the top of the coaching tree and was a reward for his hard work and constant quest to better himself. This final qualification had involved over 200 hours of study, on-line learning, conference calls and a residential study week at the University of Warwick. It covered fitness, tactics, injury prevention, agents and transfer regulations and followed B and then A licence levels. Of course coaching qualifications are only part of a successful manager's armoury but if they helped Keith move onwards and upwards in the football industry, then he was delighted he'd done it. And after all those years of looking, learning and taking everything in, he knew that if there were other ways of bettering himself then there would be no resting on his laurels, he'd seek them out and get stuck into them too.

The first game of the following season saw Keith lead his team to an impressive 4-1 home victory. A storming first half meant his lads went into the break 3-0 up, having dominated for the whole forty five minutes. Simon Yeo and Richard Butcher were among the scorers and the fans went home very happy with what they'd seen. All good stuff and another Alexander-inspired three points on the board. The only difference was that this is Peterborough United we're talking about and not Lincoln City. Although his earlier flirtation with Posh had come to nothing, Keith had subsequently decided that such a move would be a good one, and the first thing he'd done when he changed clubs was to take a couple of his old players with him.

"I had a good time at Lincoln but it was the right time to find another challenge," Keith was reported as saying. "I don't live far away, I know Barry Fry and Peterborough have potential."

"I've kept in touch with Keith ever since he left Barnet," said Fry. "He's got an eye for a player and I've always valued his knowledge. He's often recommended a player to me. Lincoln wouldn't let him come at first, but I wanted him here because he's the best person to put a team together with no money."

Barry was the owner of Peterborough and it was well documented that he'd poured every penny he'd got into keeping them afloat, including mortgaging his own house, and, as folklore would have it, his mother-in-law's too, without her knowledge.

Keith had signed a four-year contract and, inspired by his new challenge, led his new team to a healthy ten points from their first five games. They also knocked Championship side Ipswich out of the League Cup. Helen was also impressed with Keith's change of scenery.

"Keith travelled there every day and he enjoyed the new challenge," she said. "They seemed a much bigger club than Lincoln. One of the top brass at Peterborough had connections at Chelsea too. We went to see a game and stayed at the hotel there."

Most Lincoln City fans were sorry to see Keith go, but they were well used to seeing good players and good managers depart. That's the lot of fans of a lower league club. They were only too grateful for the wonderful times he had given them.

"The last time I saw Keith was in town in Lucy Tower Street multi-storey car park," said Imps fan Karl Mercer. "He was with his wife and young son and it had just been announced he was going to Peterborough. I had the opportunity to shake him by the hand and thank him for all he'd done for us and he told me he wished he'd done more. What more could he have done? He did more than most ever will."

Keith was keen to bring in his long-term colleague Gary Simpson as his deputy, but Barry Fry, now Director of Football, told him that Tommy Taylor, the former West Ham player, would be his assistant and coach. Keith therefore appointed Gary as chief scout. The club were well and truly broke, or to use a Fry-ism 'hadn't got a pot to piss in', so the management team were working under very difficult circumstances. Undeterred, the old Alexander and Simpson talent-spotting machine excelled itself again with the players they identified and brought in. George Boyd was signed from Stevenage, Aaron McLean came in from Grays Athletic and Dagenham and Redbridge were persuaded to let them have

Craig Mackail-Smith. Those three players gave the squad an extra bit of quality and it soon became apparent that they may well help the club bring in some serious funds if and when they moved onwards and upwards.

"We had no money but Keith just got on with it," said Fry. "He never moaned and the goodwill he spread around the club was brilliant. He'd got no ego and he'd spend the time talking to everyone at the club – the office staff, the shop and reception girls, the safety people – everyone. They all loved him and felt part of the team. He went out and spoke at local schools and went to local league presentation nights, all without being prompted. Even though he often lost his rag with refs, he was a guest speaker at Referees' Association meetings."

Keith may have been at a new club but the cut and thrust of football management stayed the same. The players and the surroundings might be different but he would do what he thought was right to get the best team spirit in the dressing room and the best performance he could from them when they ran out through the tunnel at five to three. Picking the team and choosing the tactics, and then guiding his men from the touchline; they too were done with the same intensity and passion. And it might be a different club he was willing on but his intolerance of poor officials remained the same. At a game at Meadow Lane, the Posh were battling it out with hosts Notts County. Literally battling it out in many ways. Leading the line for County was Jason Lee, the former Lincoln player who Keith had coached in his first spell at Sincil Bank. Lee was well known for his hairstyle during his Nottingham Forest days. It was likened to a pineapple according to some of the songs sung about him, but opposing centre-halves were far more aware of him from the bruises and broken teeth they'd suffer, having spent ninety minutes trying to mark him. It was no different here and Keith, tiring of the leniency the referee was showing to the home striker, shouted out to the official to watch him and give his players a little bit of protection. As

Peterborough attacked, Lee came over to the away dug-out and shouted to his former colleague.

"I don't know what you're moaning about Keith," he said grinning away. "All I'm doing is exactly what you fucking taught me!"

While Keith was very much in charge of the football department at London Road, the fact is that things beyond a manager's control at a club don't always stay the same and a new fresh face appeared in the Peterborough boardroom. A very powerful one. Prior to Keith's appointment, the club had been the subject of a Sky documentary entitled *Big Ron Manager*. Seen primarily as a good source of income, it proved to be an uncomfortable experience for Steve Bleasdale, the manager at the time. Former Manchester United boss Ron Atkinson played out the role of managerial troubleshooter, advising a reluctant Bleasedale while the cameras captured every cringe-worthy moment. It was so unsettling for the guy trying to pick a team and win matches that, in one episode, he even resigned on film an hour before his team kicked off in a home game. Whilst it was painful to watch for most viewers, it was said to have alerted a wealthy young man living abroad who had never previously been interested in football but who decided this was a club he might be prepared to invest in. In September, Dublin-born property entrepreneur Darragh MacAnthony arrived at London Road to open negotiations. Barry Fry had toiled for years to keep the club going and this season was no different.

"We're only getting 4,300 in the ground and we've budgeted for 5,500," he said. "I've had four years of trying to find £150,000 minimum a month to pay the wages and I'm knackered."

And so it was that MacAnthony bought Peterborough United for £1 and took on the team, the staff, the club, the ground, and, most importantly, all the debt. In his first programme notes, he said he'd spend the funds it needed to take the club from League Two to the Championship in two years.

Keith's tried and tested methods had been working well. Getting in players that no-one else had spotted and giving them a chance and building up an all-for-one team spirit had seen his side hold their own in the top third of the division. Suddenly it was different. He had money to spend. He knew if he bought new players 'off the peg' on big money it would mean dropping players who'd worked hard for him on low wages. He'd preached loyalty and now he'd be breaking his own rules. Just before he left for a business trip in America, the new chairman, already confused by his manager's lack of activity in expanding the squad, asked Keith if he would be bringing in reinforcements in the January transfer window when it arrived. Keith surprised him by saying he was happy with what he'd got. Sadly, and to make matters worse, the next six games were all lost, including a home defeat by his old club, Lincoln City, and in January 2007, MacAnthony's patience ran out.

"Darragh rang me and said we can't go on like this," said Fry. "I saw Keith on the Sunday to tell him, and again the next day. Keith was upset that he was getting the push and he was very, very disappointed. But he left with good grace and didn't blame anyone. He said he knew different owners often have different ideas."

"Barry felt terrible when he told Keith he had to go," said Helen Alexander. "He tried to make it as painless as possible. Keith was very unhappy but Barry settled up with us financially, exactly as it said in Keith's contract."

This particular owner of a football club was later quoted as saying that Keith was a lovely guy but he should have sacked him sooner. This probably rubbed salt into Keith's wounds when he felt he was doing well and needed to be left alone to do the job his way. Now, after many years managing clubs, gaining success and earning respect, he was out of work.

*****

There's an old joke, admittedly not a very good one, about a posh couple driving around in remote countryside, completely lost. They see an old ruddy-faced country yokel wearing a battered hat chewing on a piece of straw, idly leaning on a stone wall on the roadside. In exasperation they stop and ask him for directions to the destination they have been trying to find without success. The old man doesn't answer for some time and his face contorts with all the actions of someone intensely puzzled. His eyes look up and then down, and several times he seems as if he's about to answer and then stops as if correcting himself as he muses deeply over their question. Eventually, his eyes light up and he smiles as some sort of solution occurs to him, much to the relief of the weary travellers. "The best way of finding that place . . ." he says, " . . . is not to start from here." I told you it wasn't very good.

And so, after a family holiday at Disneyland Paris and a few weeks of going to games and doing the school run, Keith found himself at Bury as Director of Football. He soon discovered that he had arrived into a set of circumstances that he would have preferred not to have started from. Circumstances that were about as funny as that joke.

Chris Casper had been appointed manager at Gigg Lane in September 2005, and they'd had a torrid time. Narrowly escaping relegation from League Two in spring 2006, they followed that with another season of struggle. In addition they had been expelled from the FA Cup for fielding an ineligible player. The Bury board, to their credit, decided to show faith in Casper but brought in Keith in May 2007 to guide him. They felt that their combined efforts could bring some much needed success to the club. What they didn't do was clearly define their new management team's individual roles and that failure, combined with Casper's reluctance to accept any meaningful help from his new colleague, led to the two men having a stormy working relationship from the start.

"Chris is a young manager who has had a couple of seasons where Bury finished fourth and fifth bottom," said Keith on the club website on his arrival. "I have been in the top five or six for the last five years or so, so hopefully I can pass something on."

That public appraisal of his success and his underling's failure probably contributed to the friction that already existed between them. Privately, Keith was happy to reveal he wasn't sure of his role.

"Director of Football – that's a new one for you Keith. What exactly does it involve?" asked a former manager from their non-league days, ringing to see how he was getting on.

"Fucked if I know," replied Keith, chuckling. Of course, he'd already experienced what it felt like to seemingly have the confidence of a board who then brought someone in to help him. It had happened at Lincoln City during his first spell there. This was much more public, though, and the remit was much more vague. What he did know, however, having experienced it, was the difficulties this would present the current manager. The club's actions said to Casper, although not in so many words, that 'you haven't done a good job on your own and it doesn't look like you're going to'.

Keith's first job was to refresh the squad and bring in some new faces. He felt that one or two of his former players would be prepared to join him, so Ben Futcher and Paul Morgan were recruited to add some steel to the Bury defence. Negotiations were also underway to bring in former Lincoln and Peterborough favourite Simon Yeo to help in the goal-scoring department. Casper, already feeling threatened by Keith's appointment, then announced: "All the key decisions are mine, I am the manager, I choose the new players, pick the team and decide the tactics and the formation."

Then there was the small matter of Keith's right-hand man, Gary Simpson. Keith insisted that he was brought in, but this upset Casper even more.

"Chris thought it was two against one and he wouldn't listen to what we had to say," said Gary. "Keith should have been in a win-win situation. If Bury started winning, then Keith, and hopefully I, would have got the credit. If the bad results had continued, then Casper would go and we would take over properly. Obviously we hoped the team would perform from day one but the management structure didn't start off well at all."

Before one match, Casper told his two colleagues he wanted to hand a debut to one of the youth squad. Whilst they were never ones to hold back bringing in a youngster if he was good enough, Keith and Gary, in this instance, didn't agree and thought the lad wouldn't cope. Bury lost and the young player had a poor game. Then there were the conflicting messages that were passed to the board. On one occasion, Casper reported to them that the management trio were doing fine and Gary's contribution was a great help. The next day, Keith rang Gary to tell him that the manager couldn't work with him anymore and he'd have to go back to scouting, rather than coaching on the training ground. Once the Bury directors heard about this they were very upset, realising that they'd been deceived and their management team were far from being the happy band they'd been told they were.

"It got really bad and at one stage Casper didn't even allow Keith on the training ground," said Paul Morgan. "He didn't want him there. When Keith, Chris and the players were all together the atmosphere was terrible. I think Keith was promised certain things when he was persuaded to join the club and they never happened. He never got the chance to show what he could really do because the set-up was unworkable."

The new management structure might be failing from the start but Helen Alexander had detected a distinct advantage from her point of view.

"When Keith was at Bury, that was the only time I went to any of his games," she recalls. "He'd got a flat near the ground and we stayed there. I'd sit in the directors box and enjoy the match for once because Keith never got shouted at. He was Director of Football and Chris Casper got all the stick. Those games that Keith was involved in were the only ones I felt comfortable at."

In November, Keith and Helen received some sad news. Their good friend and Keith's former chairman at Ilkeston Town, Paul Millership, had passed away. He'd been suffering with heart and lung problems and had been found dead at his desk at home.

"He always kept in touch with Keith and had rung him when he left Peterborough," said Helen. "Keith had a club car, a Mercedes, but they took it back when he left. Paul heard he hadn't got a car so he arranged for someone to deliver a Jag for him to use. He told Keith that if he didn't get fixed up with another club he was to get himself straight back there to Ilkeston Town."

Like any good manager, Keith would never tolerate any inappropriate interference. I remember the occasion when I bumped into him as I went into the bank on Bailgate in Lincoln shortly after his dismissal from Peterborough. We went to one side and had a chat, catching up with the things each of us had been up to. I asked him about leaving London Road and he told me that the new owner had entered his office with a list of players he wanted Keith to include in the team in their next match. Smiling and anticipating the reply, I asked Keith what his response had been.

"I told him to fuck off," said Keith. "Mind you, I knew then my days were numbered," he added, smiling.

And so it was at Bury: a badly constructed managerial set-up and two, if not three, strong characters at loggerheads, feeling all the time that their methods and their ideas were being undermined.

It was hardly surprising, therefore, that the team continued to struggle and the board of directors grew more and more restless. As a winless run grew longer and longer and as the pressure from disgruntled fans mounted, they brought Keith and Chris in for a meeting. They told them they'd got a couple more games to show some signs that they could get some points on the board and get the team away from the bottom of the league. Keith protested, saying that Casper wasn't listening to what he'd advised him to do, and he should not be party to the ultimatum.

"I thought 'Oh no, here we go again'. It's Christmas and things aren't going well. Another New Year sacking is on the cards," said Helen.

Keith's protests didn't do any good and when the two games didn't bring about a win, the board sacked them both. It was early January 2008, and they left the club on the eve of an FA Cup third round replay against Norwich. A club statement announced: 'Keith and Chris had lost the confidence of a large majority of the fans'. When Alan Knill was brought in to replace them he rang Keith to ask about the squad. Keith told him that there were some good players at Gigg Lane and that had he and Gary been allowed to manage them as they'd hoped they would be, then he felt the team would be pressing for a play-off place.

So it was that Keith was sacked again and, in his opinion, unjustly again. He knew that managers didn't get that many opportunities and he wasn't sure if he'd get another one. If he did land another position it might not be in the Football League and he feared he might never work at that level again. He was very bitter because he felt he hadn't been treated fairly. He also thought that the circumstances of the last two jobs had turned out to be very different from how they'd been described. Most of all, though, he felt that after all he'd been through and after all he'd done to get himself fit enough to get back into the football industry, he'd been badly let down by it. It was a very dark time for Keith Alexander and he worried about where he'd go from here.

11

Enjoying Management at Moss Rose, the Football World Shocked

"I didn't ring him after the County game . . . I wish I had"
Matt Alexander

In the world of professional football, where money and ambition are the driving forces, it is rare to find a club that year in year out doesn't expect too much. To Macclesfield Town, being a Football League club is a mighty achievement and their main aim used to be to remain as one. Season after season they register one of the more modest average home gates in their division and quite often they have the lowest. Attendances of over 2,000 are a rarity and are more likely to result from the arrival of a sizeable number of away followers than a large amount of the good citizens of the town suddenly realising they desperately need to get down to Moss Rose to cheer the lads on.

Life is generally a bit of a battle for Macclesfield Town. After existing as a non-league club for more than 100 years, they won the GM Vauxhall Conference in the 1994-95 season only to be denied promotion to the Football League. Their ground had a capacity of less than the requisite 6,000 and it didn't have at least 1,000 seats. They won the Conference again in 1996-97 and this time were allowed to go up. This spurred them on to the greatest purple patch in the club's history because they then finished runners-up in League Three (that used to be League Four and is now League Two) and were promoted again. The next season, they enjoyed their highest ever league attendance of 6,381 when they entertained Manchester City who were coincidentally suffering the greatest slump in their history and found themselves in the third tier of English football. Sadly, the Silkmen finished bottom and have since then plied their trade in the lowest division, until their relegation in May 2012.

Lest this seems a patronising appraisal of this proud Cheshire club, it has to be said that they have always been well run, have never had to admit to crippling debts and have a neat little ground that is a credit to everyone who works there. Purely from a business point of view and their determined policy that expenditure will not exceed income, Macclesfield Town compete with difficulty against better attended or more free-spending opponents. Avoiding relegation every year was therefore rightly viewed as success. Helen Alexander was in the hairdressers when Keith rang.

"It's gone well. Very well," he told her. Then he filled her in with details of his interview with the Macclesfield board of directors before setting off on the journey home.

"We were well aware of what Keith did at Lincoln," said chairman Mike Rance. "He's got an eye for non-league talent and can work with a low budget."

The chairman and his colleagues had quickly recognised that Keith had a natural affinity with what they needed at Moss Rose. Whilst they, of course, didn't reveal it during their meeting, they were very excited that he was available and might be persuaded to join them. He was exactly the right man to take over as their manager.

"We soon realised, talking to Keith, that what you see is what you get," said Rance. "He might have had bad experiences at his last couple of clubs, but he was honest, didn't give us a load of flannel and he shot from the hip. He had a big presence and the more he spoke, the more we knew his personality would be ideal for the challenges we faced at our club."

Keith was hired until the end of the season. He understood what was demanded of him in terms of finances because Macclesfield had the lowest budget in the Football League. He was replacing Ian Brightwell and he took over with the club precariously placed only one point above the relegation zone as they entered the last quarter of the campaign.

"I soon got to know Keith well," said his new chairman. "He was a great pragmatist. He knew the boundaries as soon as he started. We knew he knew how to put a team together that would win games on the tiny budget we gave him. He knew the limitations of the job and didn't push us too far. Maybe the odd nudge now and then, but nothing hefty."

After the events at Peterborough and Bury, Keith knew that the first step to rekindling the tried and tested methods of success on a shoestring was to get Gary Simpson back as his assistant, and his old ally was quick to accept the role. On their first day in the job they met everyone connected with the club and then, with no time to lose, organised two eleven versus eleven practice games involving the first team squad and the youths. With a vitally important home game against Notts County taking place only a couple of days later, Keith was characteristically guarded about revealing his team selection. So when the team-sheets were handed around the boardroom an hour before kick-off and the starting eleven was announced over the public address system, the directors and fans were shocked to see sixteen-year-old first-year apprentice Shaun Brisley making his debut in the heart of the Macclesfield defence. Keith explained that he'd instantly seen that Brisley had got what he wanted in a defender and, using a saying that for once wasn't one of his, confirmed that 'if he's good enough, he's old enough'. The game ended 1-1 to earn the home side a valuable point and everyone agreed that local lad Brisley had played a blinder.

Another of Keith's own sayings was 'It's always nice to get a few points on the board'. As the squad listened and learned the Alexander methods, they were able to amass enough points on the board to climb the table and banish any fears of going out the Football League. A run of five wins and four draws in the last twelve games was indeed more than a few points, and everyone at Moss Rose was delighted with their new manager. The board showed their gratitude that April by offering Keith a two-year contract and, because he was back enjoying managing the way he did best, it was signed straight away.

Keith spent the summer working at keeping players at the club who he rated, moving on those he didn't and bringing in two or three who he knew and could rely on, including Simon Yeo and Paul Morgan.

"I wouldn't have signed for Bury if it wasn't for Keith being there," said Morgan. "And the same applied to my move to Macclesfield. I took a pay cut each time but I class him as both my manager and my friend and you can't put a price on that."

In July, John Rooney, brother of Wayne, signed professional terms for the Silkmen even though he had been linked with Huddersfield and Derby, and the squad gradually took shape. His chairman, like others before, soon got to know the manager's wish-list when it came to new signings. Mike Rance recalls a conversation they had one evening.

"I've seen a player I want," said Keith.

"What's he like?" asked Rance.

"He's big."

"But can he play?"

"Of course he can play, but he's big and strong, and that's just what I want," said Keith, his tone suggesting his chairman should know by now what was needed to assemble a team that could compete.

"I didn't really mix socially with Keith," said the chairman. "He lived at Dunholme in Lincolnshire with his wife and kids and stayed with friends in Buxton when the season got underway. Apart from at the club, I'd see him at golf days, that sort of thing. He was a private person – football and family were his priorities. But the work he and Gary put in was phenomenal. They went to hundreds of games, checking up on new players or to watch our up-coming opposition. Keith, Gary or both of them would ring up the office and ask us to arrange tickets for game after game, night after night. I was often tempted to tell them they should have a night off for a change. The reason I didn't mix with Keith much was because he never had time to socialise!"

"Keith would drive to Macclesfield on a Monday and come back that night," said Helen, describing the lot of a lower league manager. "Every Tuesday, he coached at the college in Lincoln if they hadn't got a midweek game. He'd go to their reserve game on a Wednesday. Then he'd drive back to Macclesfield on a Thursday and come back the next day if they were playing close to here at the weekend, or after the game on Saturday if it was at home or a long way away. He'd fit in going to lots of other games too. The club got him the use of a flat but he often stayed with our friends in Derbyshire."

The new season couldn't have started more badly. Macclesfield lost the first four games, didn't score a single goal and two of the defeats were heavy ones – 4-0 at Shrewsbury and worse still, 6-0 at home to Darlington. Then they beat Luton at home, Bournemouth away and tonked Port Vale 4-1 at home. So after a very grim start, the three-points-a-win rule meant that the club were in the top half of the table.

"We were doing a rebuilding job," said Gary Simpson. "We'd let a few players go and we'd kept faith in some of the lads who'd kept us up. We brought in one or two of our own too. Another couple were on long contracts so we had to keep them even though we didn't fancy them."

Whilst the finances were very tight, they had been improved for a period when two brothers – businessmen with local connections who joined the board with a promise of investing in the club – put in some funds at regular intervals. This lasted for a while and then stopped, and it was back to the manager and his assistant to use their original budget and generate their own funds by moving players on, loaning them out and bringing in better ones they could afford.

"The fans thought we were rolling in it and expected some quality new players," confirmed Gary. "It helped but then it dried up and we were scratching around again. Mike Rance and the board were great, though, and supported us as much as they could."

Whilst the team lost a good few games, they seemed to be able to snatch a couple of decent results just at the right time and they entered the Christmas period about halfway in League Two. Gary never ceased to keep a watchful eye on his boss's health, though.

"The gaffer was never quite the same after his illness," he observed. "He was more anxious. He used to be carefree and had everything under control. At Christmas we drove back from Morecambe where we'd lost 4-1. He shocked me by saying out of the blue that I ought to think about taking over from him at some stage. He said he still thought he was ill and he'd pack in and coach at the college or do something like that. I told him he'd regret it but he should have more time off to rest. True to form, the gaffer replied by saying that if he was the manager he couldn't be away from the club and let people down."

Like any small club, Macclesfield lived in hope that the FA Cup gods would smile on them now and again and give them a chance of glory. If they did, the money they'd get would be handy too. Usually, the main aim was getting to the third round when the big clubs entered the fray. The Silkmen weren't often seen as the favourites in a competitive game, but they overcame a potential giant-killing by winning at Harlow in the first round. Then they pulled off a tremendous 3-1 win at fellow League Two side Port Vale and they were in the hat for maybe a taste of that glory. They weren't to be disappointed when they were drawn at home to Everton and Keith, the board, the players and, last but not least, the club accountants, were all rubbing their hands with glee. A crowd of 6,332 people attended the game and Everton scraped a 1-0 win in a contest with a great atmosphere but very few chances. Everton manager David Moyes was very complimentary about his opponents and their manager and most observers concluded that there were no real losers on the day.

"Keith was very professional in how he dealt with things," his chairman was delighted to confirm. "The manager is the most important part of a club but Keith is easy to work with. We'd had managers who'd fall out with everyone every so often, so he was a breath of fresh air."

But Mike Rance was extremely worried when he walked into his manager's office at around half past one before the home game against Bournemouth in March. Keith was lying on his settee and looked ill. He confirmed he'd got a headache and he'd been sick a few minutes earlier. The club doctor arrived and took him straight off to hospital in an ambulance. Needless to say, whilst this turn of events wasn't widely known, it caused great concern among the people at the club and, of course, to his family and friends. However, after a series of scans and tests, Keith was found to be OK and, to everyone's relief, the scare was put down to a gastric bug going around Moss Rose.

"Perhaps I shouldn't have come to work that day," he told the *Macclesfield Express*. "But my generation just goes to work no matter what. You get on with it and don't make excuses. My wife wasn't very happy with me but the good news is that I'm well and have been given the all-clear."

Even so, the episode reminded everyone that Keith had been seriously ill and they needed to remember it. Rance had already been conscious of his employee's health record.

"I used to watch him on the touchline during a game," he said. "He'd be shouting at the ref and getting worked up. I'd whisper to myself 'Please be careful Keith. Be careful.'"

Macclesfield lost five games in succession in March but a victory in their last home match against Barnet and a draw at Grimsby on the last day of the season saw them safe from relegation. The rebuilding process had worked in that the club were still in the Football League – their main target. They'd got some good young prospects in the side, including Shaun Brisley who was an ever-present and had scored a few goals too. Keith and Gary had been together for a full season and their methods were working. It might not seem much, but keeping the club in the League was probably the equivalent of getting Lincoln into the play-offs or Peterborough promoted, which Keith thought he still could have done, had he been given more of a chance. He had regretted his move to Bury and the Macclesfield job had rekindled his enthusiasm for the game. It was like his time at Lincoln – he was a 'proper' manager again and he was with a club he was comfortable at, working with young players, finding new prospects and performing miracles. As the season ended, Keith was already looking forward to the next one.

However good a manager Keith Alexander was, his teams often were slow-starters. Most of his seasons at Sincil Bank had seen the team struggle early on and then go on to push for promotion. It might have been the changes he felt he needed to make each year that affected how quickly his players gelled together. It could have been the personalities of the players he signed who liked to take their time to get going and then, backs to the wall, wanted to prove people wrong. Or it could just have been coincidence. Whatever the reason, Macclesfield Town registered only one win in their first eight league games in the 2009-10 season and, for good measure, they went out of the League Cup in the first round. Then things started to click and the next eight games saw them lose only once – at home to Keith's former club Lincoln City. They were back on track and they approached Christmas away from the relegation places. Some even thought Macclesfield might just go on a bit of a run and sneak a play-off place. Domestically, Keith and Helen found that living near Lincoln and working away was good for their home life.

"One of the downsides to being manager at Lincoln," said

Helen, "was that we'd go out and he'd get asked about the club all the time. I could understand it, but he'd always get asked a question or someone would make a comment. Keith never felt comfortable unless he had a conversation with the person, because he didn't like to seem rude. We got a bit more privacy when he was Macclesfield's manager because there was less to ask him about." There was no hint of the Alexander family upping sticks and moving to Cheshire, though.

"We were really pleased with him and he was doing well," said Mike Rance. "But there was no chance of him moving here. He loved Lincoln and that's where he was going to stay. That was fine by us."

The chairman and his board backed up their support for their manager when, in January 2010, they granted Keith a two-year extension to his contract.

Eldest son Matthew was also happy living in Lincoln, to be near his father. He invited him round and often drove over to Macclesfield to see him there.

"My brother Paul and I wanted to spend more time with dad after his illness and I tried to see him as often as I could," Matthew confirmed. "I'd get him to call in and have a hot chocolate ready, along with some bourbon biscuits or ginger nuts. They were his favourites. Half the time he'd drink half a mug and jump up out of the chair saying he had to get on. He could never seem to relax. So that he had to chill out, I'd drive him to games and then he'd have to just sit there. I'd drive to Macclesfield to see him at work. I'd walk into his office and he'd be on his exercise bike watching *Golden Balls* or a cookery programme on the TV on the wall. On one occasion he drove from Lincoln to work to take training and he was then going to come back to pick me up and then drive us both down to London. We'd been invited to an awards night by the Black List, an organisation that promotes the influence of Afro-Caribbean figures in British football. I told him not to be so daft and I went over there and then drove him to the do."

Matthew had moved back to Lincolnshire from London

and, while he was still registered as a player's agent, had greatly reduced his workload.

"I realised when dad was ill that there's more to life than business and chasing deals. I used to work endless hours as an agent and freelancing for other sports agencies. Mind you, we had some great conversations about the levels of money in the game, especially the contrast in earnings between guys I'd dealt with and the players in his squad. I once arranged a boot deal for a Brazilian international playing in the Premier League. He got 1,000,000 Euros for it. That was about one and a half times the entire budget dad had got for his squad for the season. I used to get invited to some amazing events and I tried to involve my dad if I could. I wanted to spoil him. I was asked to go to a small dinner party and a top England international and a celebrity TV chef were going to be there. I made a couple of calls and arranged it so that dad could be there too. He said he'd come but cried off at the last minute. I think he was a bit nervous about going. He went to a Macclesfield Town auction night instead."

The broader subject of black managers was often brought up in interviews with Keith. It was a change from questions about more immediate matters such as his team and their results. He recalled his first stint as a League manager back in 1993.

"There were two black managers then, including me," he was quoted as saying. "And here we are in 2010 and it's still just two. Twenty per cent of players are black, yet there's only two managers out of ninety two clubs. There are no black people at the top level at the FA, the Football League or the Premier League."

Macclesfield went into 2010 on a run of only one defeat in six games. Never one to miss an opportunity to strengthen the team, Keith went about recruiting a player who would be good for the squad but who was also a very good friend. Richard Butcher's career had stalled after the highs of his first stint at Lincoln City. He'd gone to Oldham and had a terrible time. The fans there couldn't have viewed him more differently than Lincoln supporters had done, and the boo boys gave him relentless criticism. Keith rescued him by signing him for Peterborough and then he'd had two seasons with Notts County. In his third spell at Lincoln, the mutual trust, respect and friendship he'd had with Keith was a distant memory when compared to his relationship with current manager Chris Sutton. Butcher cut a sad figure and a shadow of the athletic goal-scoring midfielder from the play-off days when Sutton reluctantly gave him some first team action. Those chances were usually from the bench when Sutton's poorly-organised and struggling side was already losing. Keith knew what was happening and arranged a loan deal that brought Richard to Moss Rose. As if the weight was already lifted from his shoulders, he scored on his debut for his new side at Bury, although his goal turned out to be a consolation in a 2-1 defeat.

The team had a habit of nicking a few points just when the fear of relegation might rear its ugly head and, when they took the lead and were in control at Bournemouth in February, it looked like they were going to do it again. Then, with a few minutes to go, the Macclesfield keeper was well and truly clattered and the home team scrambled the ball home to equalise.

"Keith had a real go at the referee, the assistant referee and the fourth official," said Mike Rance. "So much so, the ref sent him off and he had to come up into the stand to sit with us. He was very, very upset."

The club received the FA disciplinary papers for Keith's dismissal a week or so later and they needed to decide if he would attend a hearing. If so, he might have been a little hard to understand because at the same time he had developed a bout of hiccups that wouldn't go away. Despite its comedic affect, it was actually something that worried Keith and Helen because any change in his health, even a quirky one such as this, might just be related to his previous problems.

The hospital quickly arranged for tests to be carried out to make sure it wasn't.

Macclesfield had a midweek away game against Notts County and Keith drove with Richard Butcher, another Lincoln resident, the short distance to Meadow Lane. It was a bit of a homecoming for Keith and, although the main priority was to try and get a result against their high-flying opponents, he was looking forward to seeing a lot of friends there. Mike Rance took along the disciplinary papers for Keith to sign after the match to make sure that they didn't fall foul of the FA deadlines. When it came to expenditure on players, it was a real David against Goliath contest and, despite a good showing, Macclesfield lost 1-0 to their more illustrious opponents.

Tony Cuthbert had been secretary at Ilkeston when Keith started his managerial career there and he was now in that position at Notts County, so they were delighted to meet up in the boardroom for a chat. Tony's two sons, Lee and Ryan, had loved being involved at Ilkeston and now, years later, still felt great affection for Keith. True to form, he spotted Lee in the crowd while Macclesfield warmed up and he went over to shake his hand and exchange a few quick words. After the game, everyone in the bar and the boardroom wanted to speak to Keith and, although he was disappointed with the result, he didn't let them down and was happy to chat away. Late on, as the Macclesfield contingent left for the return journey and people eventually drifted away, Mike Rance and Keith, in his car with Richard, headed off in opposite directions. Rance, sighing, realised they'd forgotten to deal with those infernal forms.

"Me again," said the chairman, ringing from his car. "We forgot you needed to sign that paperwork. I know you're not at the club tomorrow Keith, so can you get yourself near a fax in the morning?"

"Yes chairman, no problem. We'll sort it out tomorrow," replied his manager and he resumed chatting to his player and friend as they made their way home.

*****

Some people have some strange ideas about where it's possible to build a new house. I'd driven from Lincoln up to the outskirts of Scunthorpe to look at a potential site for one of our customers and, as soon as I got there, could see that it was about as unsuitable as you could get for building a new dwelling and then living there. I walked back to the car muttering Meldrew-esque curses about time-wasters under my breath, tempered only by the knowledge that I was going to meet my middle son for a round of golf at Gainsborough on the way back.

"... was fifty-three and had been manager of Macclesfield Town for the last two years ..." Radio Five Live said as soon as I turned on the ignition. For one split second I thought 'that's Keith – has he got another manager's job?' Then, a further split second later, it came to me that saying: "was fifty-three" wasn't the language used by a sports reporter telling his listeners about a new football appointment. Tuning in to more local stations I then quickly realised the awful news. The big man was dead.

"I'd got home from work early," said John Cockerill. "A mate rang and said 'It's terrible news about Keith isn't it?' I just said 'What news?' and, knowing then that I hadn't heard, he apologised and told me he'd passed away. I dived in the car straightaway and drove to Dunholme to see Helen and the kids."

"I got a call from Matt at about 8.00 a.m. He told me what had happened," said Mike Rance. "That chat Keith and I had about the FA form the night before was the last time I spoke to him. I was devastated. Straightaway people started bringing flowers and tributes to the ground."

"I spoke to Keith late on after the game at Meadow Lane, at about half eleven," Gary Simpson explained. "We talked about getting a player in to cover for Izak Reid, who was injured. He said he was going to watch John Rooney who was on trial at Derby and was playing for their reserves next day. I knew something was wrong when Matt rang me the next morning. He told me what had happened. At the time, the gaffer was still with us, but Matt explained it was only a matter of time."

I rang my lad and told him I wouldn't be golfing. At home, I made a couple of calls and then sat and watched the sports channel on television or listened to the radio as they reported the news and interviewed people who spoke emotionally about the man they knew. It transpired Keith had become unwell when he got home and after collapsing was taken to Lincoln County Hospital where he died. His next game would have been his 100th as manager of Macclesfield. As interview followed interview and tribute followed tribute that afternoon and in the days ahead, it soon became clear that it wasn't just the rarity of the death of a current manager that led so many people to express their sadness. It was a reflection of the respect and affection that a huge amount of people felt for him. Clearly, some of the most poignant comments came from those who were closest to Keith.

"I never rang my dad before a game. It was a superstition we had," said Matt Alexander. "I didn't even ring him at Celtic Manor before the play-off final. If I saw him before a match it was OK. I didn't see him before the game at Meadow Lane, though, because I'd been out shopping with Remi, my little girl, and I needed to get her home. We often chatted after a match when he was on the team bus or driving back to Lincoln. I didn't ring him after the Notts County game because it was late. I wish I had because later that night he was dead."

12

Recognition and Reflections

"He was a splendid man"
Gary Simpson

A bitterly cold wind blew on the morning of Monday 15th March, when the doors of Lincoln Cathedral were opened for the funeral of Keith Alexander. Family members, friends, players, managers, supporters, representatives from football authorities and well-wishers gradually arrived and took their places inside the great building or out in the grounds. Thousands of people were there.

On the day Keith died, clubs where he had worked, including Lincoln City, Grimsby Town and Macclesfield Town, opened their gates for fans to lay flowers and memorabilia in his memory. The England national team played at Wembley against Egypt that evening and wore black armbands as a tribute to him. England Under-21s took on Greece and did the same. Players at clubs all over the country wore them too at domestic matches the weekend after his passing and matches were preceded with either a minute's silence or a minute's applause. Macclesfield Town did not play that Saturday. It was too soon. Fittingly, they won their first game after their manager had died, away at Hereford, and the players wore special shirts with 'Rest in Peace Gaffer' printed on the back. Throughout the game, Silkmen fans chanted Keith's name and Gary Simpson and the players dedicated the win to him.

"Today was Keith's day," said Richard Butcher. "There are a few tears in that dressing room and we are proud we got the win for him."

At Lincoln City's home game against Hereford, many kind words were said and deeds done to recognise the club's former manager. The match programme was largely dedicated to him and included archive photos, details of his career and articles about him by friends and colleagues from the past. A series of pages entitled 'Remembering Keith' featured quotes from over eighty people from every part of the football world who knew Keith and were pleased to express their thoughts about him.

On the 13th of March, two days before the funeral, Macclesfield played at Moss Rose for the first time since losing Keith. Before they kicked off against Bury, tributes were made by representatives of the six clubs he had managed and fifty three doves – one for each year of Keith's life – were released. Fittingly again, the Silkmen won the game.

Many well-known faces from the world of football could be seen inside Lincoln Cathedral when the service began, including Martin O'Neill, Mick McCarthy, Chris Hughton, Les Ferdinand, Paul Ince, David Moyes, Chris Powell and Sir Trevor Brooking. Everyone who knew Keith, whether professionally or personally, seemed to be there. For example, every single member of the Stamford squad who appeared at Wembley all those years ago, except for two who had died at tragically early ages, was there. As the doors opened for the coffin to arrive, those seated could hear the sound of applause from the people assembled outside. The coffin bearers included Gary Simpson, Keith's long-time colleague and friend, and John Cockerill, his good pal. Son Paul delivered a tribute, brother Randall read a poem, hymns were sung and two of Keith's favourite songs – *Mr Bojangles* and *No Woman No Cry* – were performed by pupils from Lincoln Minster School. Macclesfield chairman Mike Rance spoke impressively as he described Keith.

"Speaking at the funeral was the hardest thing I've ever had to do," he recalls. "I'm told there were 2,000 people in the cathedral and 1,000 outside. It was a great privilege to speak but I was terrified because I didn't want to let Keith down." He certainly didn't.

The Bishop of Lincoln, Dr John Saxbee, spoke characteristically skilfully and humorously when he described Keith. He reminded us that whenever his first name was uttered, everyone knew who was being discussed. He described Keith's personality, his skills and the way he overcame challenges purely by the force of his own character. He even said Keith was "one hell of a manager." Applause rang around the cathedral for a second time when the coffin was carried out. After the service in Lincoln, Keith was buried at Dunholme church following a short ceremony involving a small group of family and close friends.

"The funeral in the cathedral was incredible," said John Cockerill. "But the ceremony at Dunholme felt more like Keith's style. I don't mean that in a bad way. It was wonderful how many people came. But laying him to rest with only a few of us there seemed right. To everyone, he was just Keith, a big man who never wanted any fuss."

In the days and weeks that followed, many more tributes and displays of recognition took place, whether large or small. Piara Power, director of the Kick It Out anti-racism campaign, praised Keith for his trail-blazing achievements. Richard Bevan, Chief Executive of the League Managers Association, confirmed that Keith was being put forward for a position on their executive board around the time he passed away. The FA Head of Coaching, John Peacock, said that Keith had gained all his coaching qualifications and had then asked about becoming a licensed FA Tutor at some stage. He said the FA would have most probably agreed to his request because he was skilled enough to be someone who coached coaches.

The Sacred Sports Foundation in St Lucia, of which Keith was a director, continued to carry out its work. The Black List, which is backed by the FA, the PFA and Kick It Out movement, honoured Keith with a posthumous lifetime achievement award at a celebratory evening at Wembley. Locally, events were held and funds raised. Donations at the funeral and afterwards were held in trust ready for a decision being made on which charity or organisation would receive them. Former clubs of Keith's and fans all over the country collected money for a variety of causes. Ilkeston Town held a golf day, with proceeds going to Keith's memorial fund. In addition to events and charitable collections, decisions were made to preserve Keith's name at a range of venues. The bar for home and visiting fans in the relatively new Henshaw's Stand at Macclesfield's Moss Rose ground was renamed the 'Keith Alexander Bar'. The 'Goals at Cherry' facility at Cherry Willingham school, near Lincoln, which comprises pitches, changing rooms and a learning suite was re-christened the 'Keith Alexander Football Centre'.

In April, Gary Simpson was appointed as permanent manager of Macclesfield Town and given a two-year contract. As caretaker-manager, he'd battled through a terribly difficult time with great dignity. His football philosophy and his close partnership with Keith over the years made him the natural successor to his great friend. It would be Gary, therefore, who would have to meet the challenges that Keith so capably dealt with in taking their small club forward. At the ground, the fans had set up a tribute in a stand which remained there for months. Chairman Mike Rance readily admitted to regularly being upset by it as he tried hard to concentrate on all the day-to-day duties that had to be carried out.

The Lincolnshire Echo ran a feature highlighting some of Keith's quotes during his time at Sincil Bank. It was a novel way of reminding its readers how he was never reluctant to speak his mind.

"I want to play good football but you have to change your style to suit your circumstances. You can't get good footballers on £250 a week," he said about his style of play. "The only reason they criticise us is that we have a player who is 6'4" in Ben Futcher who we send up for throw-ins, free-kicks and corners. But why not? They don't like it because they can't defend against it. They can keep on moaning because we'll be doing it for the rest of the season," he said, when opposing managers complained about one of his tactics. Following racist abuse received by England players Emile Heskey and Ashley Cole, he told a reporter: "I know if any of our players were abused during a league game I would take the team off. There would be no hesitation on my part." And following the play-off defeat against Grimsby which turned out to be his last game in charge of Lincoln, he said: "Who knows what's around the corner? Whatever happens, Lincoln City will go on whether Keith Alexander is here or not".

On 3rd May, a benefit match took place at Sincil Bank in memory of Keith and to celebrate his life. Barry Fry was among the organisers and a Keith Alexander side managed by Gary Simpson took on an all-stars squad managed by Paul Ince. The souvenir programme, like many of those prepared for games involving clubs with an Alexander connection, was filled with tributes about him. Fry, members of Keith's family, Gary Simpson, representatives from Lincoln, Peterborough, Bury, Macclesfield, the League Managers Association, the Sacred Sports Foundation and people from his non-league playing days all contributed articles describing their relationship with Keith and their appreciation of him as a colleague and a friend. Over forty other people were quoted in the programme, expressing the shock they felt at his demise and their fond memories of him over the years. Most of the squad that took Lincoln City to the Millenium Stadium on two occasions played for the Keith Alexander team, including Alan Marriott, Jamie McCombe, Paul Morgan, Stuart Bimson, Mark Bailey, Simon Weaver, Ben Futcher, Ben Sedgemore, Simon Yeo and Gareth McAuley. Other Lincoln City favourites were there too, either playing or watching. The all-stars team included Paul Merson, Jimmy Floyd Hasselbank, Rob Lee, Dion Dublin, Les Ferdinand and player-manager for the day, Paul Ince. In amongst the large crowd sat Helen Alexander, children Jack and Jenny and other members of Keith's family. It was a moving but uplifting afternoon.

*****

I make no apologies for describing at some length the strength of feeling caused by Keith's passing, or the events that took place to commemorate him and celebrate his achievements. Equally, I am not sorry to refer to the hundreds of tributes that were made by people who knew him, either well-known themselves or from more modest walks of life. I haven't quoted verbatim every single one because that would fill a whole book. Maybe, however, the thoughts of some of those who were closest to him in the game he loved might be the best way to conclude this part of his biography. Their inclusion might appear gloomy or morbid – I hope not – but they give us another way to find out even more about the man himself. They reveal in a positive way his methods, his management style and his personality.

"I was chairman of Cliftonville when Keith joined us," says Jim Boyce, now president of the club and a FIFA vice-president. "We needed to finish in the first eight because the league was being split at the end of the season and the top eight would stay in the top division. After his first game, the 4-3 win over Portadown, I got everyone asking me where I got him from and could I get any more like him. He soon became a cult figure and I'd kept in touch with him ever since. When Keith was at Ilkeston, I rang him to say we needed a 'keeper. He put a non-league lad, Paul Reece, in touch with us. Paul played for us for a few games, then stayed on for the next full season when we won the league for the first time in seventy eight years. Keith had recommended a goalkeeper to us who kept nineteen clean sheets in one season. It showed he knew his stuff when it came to recognising talent. At one stage, Keith was interested in moving to Northern Ireland to work as a development officer. We needed six officers to coach coaches throughout the country. He was thinking of coming but then got the Lincoln job."

"Keith was an affable guy," says Steve Thompson, his boss at Lincoln City. "He had time for everyone. He was serious when he needed to be but was great fun too when things were more relaxed. As youth coach, he was great with the younger players. He came into League football late and kept telling them how lucky they were to be at a club and how they shouldn't waste the chance they'd got. Taking over from me as manager came too soon for him. He went off and learned his trade in non-league. After he was ill the first time, I told him he should look to be a director at an academy – something like that. You can't switch off when you're a manager. But once you put the grease paint on and walk on to that stage you can't give it up."

Andy King was his manager at Mansfield Town where Keith played and, as assistant, did just about everything else too.

"Keith knew the game," he says. "He was a good judge and a great coach. He didn't have to be the centre of attention. He had a presence just by being there."

"Keith learned his trade. He played, he coached, he got his qualifications, he scouted, he managed," says Adie Boothroyd, a fellow player at Mansfield and now Northampton manager, and who always kept in touch with him. "He worked harder than just about everyone. It was nothing about him being black that he got on and won everyone's affection and respect. It was because he was good at his job and because he was a good man. Everyone says how nice he was, which was true. But he had a lovely wicked sense of humour. If anyone tried to have a go, he could cut them to shreds with his humour. He was a great guy."

"Keith wasn't great in the air for a tall lad," says former Grimsby Town team-mate Gary Birtles. "But he had huge desire and was fantastic at holding the ball up for midfielders to run on to. As a manager he was a nice guy but had steel when it was needed. He could be hard on some players but would have a quiet word if that went down better. Just like Brian Clough was when I was at Forest. He was a funny man and a mean poker player. He was natural and never forgot his roots. Keith was a stunning human being."

It has already been mentioned how Keith had quite an impact during his brief spell in Northern Ireland with Cliftonville.

"I can still see his goals now," says Marty Quinn, who was their manager at the time. "I remember one game when he was through on goal with only a huge big Scottish keeper to beat. I thought he'd over-run the ball and left himself too much to do, but he scored. After the game, he casually said 'No bother boss, I'd got it under control.'"

"Not only did he score on his debut, but his ability, experience and guidance helped transform our season," says Cliftonville chairman Gerard Lawler. "We all remember his great goals and the great nights. He was always a friend to our club."

People who met Keith during his non-league management days were pleased to recall their involvement with him.

"I played for Ilkeston Town during the most successful time in the club's history," says John Knapper. "You couldn't wish to play for a better manager."

Dave Thomas was secretary at Northwich Victoria. "The club was in complete disarray when he arrived here. He worked wonders to keep us up. Most people remember him for the FA Cup run, though. We had a televised game that brought us in a huge sum of money and he was gutted when we lost and missed out on the tie against Spurs. He made a lot of friends in the non-league scene."

"I spoke to Keith about him being my assistant," says Neil Warnock, who has managed clubs at all levels from non-league through to the Premier League. "He thought seriously about it but was then offered another job as a number one. He was a gentle giant who always had a good word for people."

Andy Farrant was a local radio reporter when Keith was manager at Sincil Bank first time round. "I worked at Radio Lincolnshire and then left to work at the World Service for a longish period," he recalls. "I came back to the station in Lincoln years later. I bumped into Keith and he recognised me and chatted with me like I'd never been away."

Two individuals, Grant Brown and John Schofield, had more football connections with Keith Alexander than anyone else. In three consecutive years they played against him when Lincoln City met Grimsby Town, played with him when he joined them at Sincil Bank and the following season played under him when he was made manager. Brown also later coached with him at Lincoln in the early 2000s and was a coach for the club when they took on Macclesfield Town, led by Keith, in recent times.

"He knew how to make people feel part of a team," says Brown. "Not just football people, but fans, staff and everyone. It was part natural – he was a nice guy – but it was also an intentional way of building a team spirit throughout the playing squad and the club as a whole. To show how nice he was – I had made more appearances for Lincoln than anyone in their history. He took over at the club from Alan Buckley and told me I was being released. And I still liked him! These days we all miss him. I just remember him smiling, those big white teeth, standing on the touchline in his long coat, baseball cap and those trademark yellow socks."

A fellow manager had very personal reasons to be grateful to Keith. "Keith's sister helped me organise my marriage in St Lucia," explains Russell Slade, now at Leyton Orient. "Keith was out there that particular week and I asked him to be my best man. He said 'no problem' and we had a terrific time. Keith's uncle performed the ceremony but they hadn't seen each other for a few years, so he kept stopping the proceedings to have a chat with my best man. It was quite bizarre really! I knew Keith for over twenty years and he was a football and family man. But he was also a fighter. One of his sayings that he said to everyone was 'I'm keeping my head above water'. That was his way of saying things were tough but he was going to keep going."

The relationship between a manager and the local media is always finely balanced. They need each other: the media to tell their stories and the manager to get his message across to the fans and everyone else at his club. If either gets it wrong, like when a news item goes out that gives away a secret or a manager isn't as accessible as he should be, then the balance is wrong and the relationship tipples over.

"Keith told me a lot of stuff off the record so that I was kept informed," says local radio sports reporter Michael Hortin. "He never got upset about reports about himself. He developed the Team Lincoln thing, which included the players of course and the club staff, but everyone else too, including the local media. His only Achilles heel was people getting at his players. He wouldn't stand for that. Everyone at Radio Lincolnshire loved him for the way he was." Hortin also recognised how astute Keith was at reading the game. "Between his Peterborough and Bury jobs, he would come along and summarise at a few Lincoln City games," he explains. "He went with me to Walsall and while I did the commentary, he'd contribute some expert comments. Lincoln won to go top and Spencer Weir-Daley got both goals. Driving back in the car he surprised me by saying that Lincoln had done very well so far but would falter as the season reached its climax. He said that, although they were top of the league, the team and the tactics were getting found out. He thought the system they were using would be easy to stop. He was spot-on. They did falter and went from top to limping into the play-offs where they were easily beaten. He certainly knew his stuff."

"Keith always had time for me," says *Lincolnshire Echo* reporter Leigh Curtis "And he couldn't have been more helpful. He had his cataracts done – 'Keith's vision for the game' was our corny headline when we ran the story – and he invited me to his house when he came out of hospital. He was in his slippers watching cricket when I got there. He got straight up saying he was going to make me a cup of tea. He was just out of hospital and his eyes were very sore. There he was, looking after a football reporter. How many managers would do that? Then there was the time our daughter, Lottie, was born. Matt Alexander came round with a bottle of pink champagne saying it was from his dad and him. I've still got it – it was too nice a gesture to open it and drink it. He was great to interview but he always wanted the players to get the credit. 'They were magnificent from start to finish' was one of his sayings."

Mike Rance, chairman at Macclesfield, gives an insight into the chairman-manager relationship he had with Keith. "He was an absolute pleasure to work with and be with," he says. "Honest and pragmatic, knowledgeable and hard-working, he first stabilised a club on the brink and then set out to build a team that would beat the odds. Keith and Gary were very much like Brian Clough and Peter Taylor – Keith the charismatic one and Gary the one who made Keith's wishes happen."

Of all the people in football who come into contact with a manager, it is the players who make or break him. And vice versa. How he deals with them and how they respond is everything. Keith's players at Lincoln City all have stories to tell about him that show how significant he was in their careers in particular and their lives in general.

"I can only thank him for the six best years of my life. He made my career," says midfielder Peter Gain succinctly. "Keith Alexander was the only manager in football who could pull you into his office, tell you you're not playing and you came out with a smile on your face," said Ben Futcher. "That's just the type of guy he was."

Simon Yeo was with the club when the finances were dire. "We never had any money but we had the laughs and the team spirit that were second to none," he remembers. "If any of the lads had personal problems, Keith would understand and he'd let you have time off if you needed it. He was a father figure and approachable. You wanted to play and win for him, not for yourself."

Goalkeeper Alan Marriott reveals how concerned he was when Keith was ill. "A lot of people told him that he shouldn't have carried on after such a serious illness but people who knew him knew that football was the only thing he ever wanted to do. He would go from watching a Premier League game right down to standing on the touchline at a Sunday League game. He loved football that much. Being in that squad was like having a kick-around with your mates. When you play with your mates you want to give that extra effort and that's what happened under Keith."

"He was the nicest guy I ever met in football," says defender Paul Mayo. "I've played for some pretty horrible managers, but he was the best. I left Lincoln once and then came back because of him."

Striker Francis Green played under Keith's leadership at Ilkeston, Lincoln and Macclesfield. "We had our ding-dongs but they never affected the relationship we had," says Green. "He would be my biggest admirer and my biggest critic because we were close. His man-management was great. Over the years there were many times I'd go and see him and he would have time to listen and help. I owe him everything as a player."

Midfielder Ben Sedgemore was another who knew Keith well before he signed for him at Lincoln. "I first met Keith as a seventeen-year-old," he recalls. "My Birmingham youth team played Lincoln's youngsters under Keith's lead. He was instrumental in taking me to Mansfield with him and Andy King. He used to say 'We're a good team with good players who know what we are about' in every pre-match team talk. In my time at Lincoln he took a gang of misfits and reprobates and moulded them into a team. Like Alf Ramsey, he didn't just pick the best players, he picked the best players for the team. He also had the vision and confidence to challenge convention. I have still never seen another team send the centre-back, Ben Futcher in our case, up the pitch to flick on our own goal-kicks. Keith knew it worked and we trusted his judgement."

A lot of players who worked under Keith went on to bigger and better things. Gary Taylor-Fletcher starred for Blackpool in the Premier League in the 2010-11 season, having scored in the Championship play-off final to help get them there. He remains the only player to have scored in all of the top six divisions in the English football pyramid.

"I was going nowhere until I met Keith," he says. "I was going to college and working in a bar. Years later I'm in the Premier League and the one person I can thank for that is Keith. He saw me at Northwich and gave me a chance. Then he took over at Lincoln City and rescued me from a bad time I was having at Orient. When I was at Lincoln, every ground we went to he said he'd scored at. He always said it. We used to laugh at him and say, according to him, he must have scored at every ground in the country. He was a great bloke. Ninety-nine per cent of my progress in football is down to him."

Of all the players who were managed by Keith Alexander, his former captain, Paul Morgan, probably had the most contact with him. The manager and captain relationship is very important but Morgan's recollections of him and his team-mates include some experiences well away from football that were a significant part of his boss's management style.

"Keith encouraged us all to go out together on a Tuesday and Saturday night," he explains. "He loved the fact that we'd go out and enjoy ourselves because he knew that our bond would just get stronger. We were always under strict instructions not to cause trouble and we never did because we had too much respect for him. I know he used our nights out as a selling point to other players he wanted to sign. I've been at a few clubs since and the camaraderie we had at Lincoln has never been replicated. As players we may have gone our separate ways but we keep in touch and meet up all the time."

Morgan is equally complimentary about Keith's methods at building a team that won games. "He made sure we enjoyed our football. He was wrongly labelled a long-ball exponent. We were direct sometimes but our creative play in the opposition box took some defending against. There were no individuals, no stars; we were all a team. He treated younger players just the same as the senior ones. He dealt with winning or losing just the same. He had charisma and he greeted you every Monday with a big smile – whether we'd won or lost. He just encouraged and advised. As others might say too, he even had a knack of dropping you and you didn't mind. I don't think he got the recognition he deserved."

One player out of all of those who served under Keith Alexander personified his style and mirrored his personality more than most. Richard Butcher developed as a superb athlete and a fine footballer in his first spell at Lincoln City. But more than that, he was an integral part of the team spirit that was formed at the time – a spirit that was forged on friendship, hard work, respect for others and enjoying life with all its twists and turns. Richard would have loved to contribute to this book, to the story of his good friend, and he no doubt would have struggled to describe that last car journey he had with Keith as they travelled back from Nottingham. Sadly, as we all know, Richard was to pass away too, and many people still cannot believe that both their favourite manager and their favourite player are no longer around. After Keith's death, Richard spoke warmly about him.

"He simply knew how to get the best out of me," he said. "His man-management was exceptional and he knew if he had a squad of only twenty, he couldn't treat them all the same. He was my boss but my friend too. We used to travel to Macclesfield together and there would never be any awkward silences. The best times I had as a player were under him and it's funny but we both agreed that our time at Lincoln in the play-off years were the best of our careers."

"He was a great family man and I couldn't have had a better best mate," says close friend John Cockerill. "As a manager he was very thorough and very determined. It's a shame he never managed a really big club because he would have done well. He was knowledgeable and worked very long hours. Although he was a jovial character he never sought the limelight."

Finally, the views of the man who worked most closely with Keith perhaps give the clearest insight into him. Gary Simpson was part of a small team of two that gathered up a collection of unknowns, rejects even some of them, and made them into a team with that all-for-one spirit. Then they sent them into battle and, more often than not, it seemed like they'd got a one-man or a two-man advantage. Never one to use two words when one would do, Gary puts it quite simply: "Keith was larger than life. An honest man. In the difficult times we had, we helped each other through things and he was just a rock. I never saw a weak streak in him. He was a splendid man."

*****

As a player, Keith Alexander didn't let the grass grow under his feet. He played for lots of clubs and each change of scenery was down to him. He kept moving, kept learning. Almost without exception, his former club would try to persuade him to stay when he told them he was setting off to a new one. They didn't succeed but there was no resentment, only good memories. Keith probably learned most from his first taste of management at Lincoln City. After that, he decided what his methods would be; he built up his network of allies in the game; and he learned how to build a team on the pitch and a team throughout a club off it. As he progressed and became better known, he resolutely remained true to his roots. He was proud of where he came from and he kept in touch with people from his past because he liked them. His famous yellow socks, worn every time he watched his side from the touchline, were part of his FA Vase-winning kit with Stamford. He wore them to bring him luck, but they were also a fond reminder of a good time he'd enjoyed years earlier with a good gang of people.

Qualifications weren't thought of as a tiresome necessity, they were another opportunity to learn and advance. For all this gathering of knowledge and experience, Keith didn't want to copy anyone else. He wanted to do things his way and, whilst always remaining polite and courteous, he wouldn't suffer fools gladly.

As a manager, his style of play would be questioned and sometimes criticised. It's true he often employed a high-tempo direct approach that might wear down more accomplished sides that had been put together with better resources. That's the point really. He used that style because he had to employ low-paid but keen young lads who relished a chance at playing for him and against bigger clubs. But this 'direct' label was a bit unfair because when the system worked and the results were good, the flowing football followed. Those same young men playing to simple instructions grew in confidence and started to try more adventurous things. They were encouraged to do so. Plenty of fans of clubs Keith had managed would dispute the 'long ball' label their side had acquired when they recollect some of the great performances and exciting times they'd enjoyed with him directing things from the touchline.

Another label Keith picked up was how he was the expert at making a 'silk purse out of a sow's ear'. Everyone said he could create a team that cost next to nothing, but maybe he wasn't so good at splashing the cash when he'd got a chairman or a board with lots of money and even more ambition. For a start, Ilkeston Town under Alexander and Millership were a big fish in a small pond. It might only have been down in the lower reaches of non-league, but the principle was still the same. They had more money than most and it meant most other clubs wanted to beat them because of it. Keith put together a good team on a healthy budget for that level and they had some good seasons. That club had just as much team ethic and togetherness as the less well-off ones he managed.

At Peterborough United, the new money that became available to him after a period of scrimping and saving was well meant but came at the wrong time. He could have agreed to those generous offers and brought in highly paid players on big wages. But he'd built a team, they were doing OK, and he had to stay loyal to them for his plans to work. Anything else would have been wrong. The respect and the loyalty he was getting in return would have gone at a stroke. Better that players played for him and had the chance to succeed with him than players who came in and played first and foremost for a fat wage packet every week and a hefty bonus every game. The gradual introduction of higher profile guys into the squad, coupled with improvements to the lot of ones already there, would have worked, but he wasn't asked to do that. In fact, as he confirmed later, he was being told rather than asked, and that didn't help either.

That leads into the next question. Would Keith have been able to manage at a higher level? He probably missed his chance by sticking to his principles at London Road. That isn't to say that he might not have been attracted away from Macclesfield if his good work there had continued and been spotted by someone wanting something similar a couple of divisions higher. Keith knew players and he knew how to galvanise a club. Who's to say he couldn't have done that in, say, the Championship? A small club there, taking on much bigger ones with Premier League ambitions. A lot of people would think he would have done well at that level. What Keith promoted was the way to play to your strengths. Accept your limitations and plan what would upset the opposition. What Keith was good at might even apply at the highest level, if the people up there were prepared to try it.

In the Premier League less than forty per cent of players

are English. A lot of them are good but not great. The players that excite and make things happen every Saturday, or more likely every Sunday, are predominantly foreign, and fair play to them. Yet every English manager tries to get every England team to pass and move and take on more gifted opponents at their own game. We pass it around the back, realise there's nothing on and float it up and over a lone striker's head. Playing fast, closing down, putting them under pressure and getting behind their defence. That would work and the fans would love it too. A recent England manager earned 200 times more in a year than Keith Alexander did when he got Lincoln City to Cardiff's Millennium Stadium, and that is no particular criticism of that national coach because he'd managed at the highest club level and was the best candidate at the time. He didn't know how to unsettle better teams and beat them though, like Keith did, and the principle is still the same whatever level you manage at.

As a player and a manager, Keith had some weaknesses. As a player he had no mean streak at all. He might have done better on the pitch if he had, and he might have played for better clubs, too, by turning it on when he knew someone influential was watching. When the boots had been hung up and he moved into coaching and management, maybe he was prone to persuasion a few times. If he liked someone, he might just have been a bit too friendly and agreed to things that maybe he shouldn't have, like the Peterborough jolly. One thing is for sure, he wouldn't be told what to do by anyone he didn't respect. If they said do this or that, and he didn't agree, they soon knew about it.

Whoever Keith worked for, his relationship with his players was his first priority and he would always be loyal to them, sometimes to the point of getting himself into a little bit of trouble. In a game at Chester, Lincoln City captain Paul Morgan was sent off. His frustration at a series of poor decisions led him to raise his hands and give the referee a shove. After the game, Keith told the *Lincolnshire Echo* he could understand his skipper's actions because the referee "was useless and shouldn't be allowed on a pitch again." A couple of days later, the paper's football reporter Leigh Curtis got a phone call.

"Keith said the Football Association were unhappy with his comments," said Leigh. "They were taking action. He asked if I could ring them and tell them I'd misquoted him. I was a bit reluctant but before I could say 'no', he told me he'd already told them I'd admitted it and would be getting in touch. Quite honestly, I was pleased to help Keith so I rang the FA guy. Before I could finish saying I'd got my story a little bit wrong, the bloke sighed, as if he knew what was going on and, in a resigned tone, said he wouldn't be taking any more action. Keith and I had a little chuckle about it when we next met up."

That was Keith. He would say that his team would be there or thereabouts when he was asked about their chances of success. When it came to his achievements and the way he worked, he was certainly there or thereabouts in the higher reaches of the managers' league table. But when it came to some of the rules and the strictures of the game, especially the ones that didn't seem to achieve anything, he was more thereabouts than there. He couldn't be doing with unnecessary conventions. He did things his way and most of the time that was so that he could give his players the best chance possible or he could take his club one step further. When you are determined and you know you are doing the right thing, you don't need some pointless officialdom getting in the way.

As his story reaches its end and readers reflect on Keith Alexander's life, there's one conclusion that is beyond doubt. He blew out of the water the theory that being a decent bloke doesn't get you anywhere in the harsh world of professional football. Being nice but pretending to be hard, or already being hard and acting like a bully, will get you short-term gains. But Keith showed that being a nice guy built friendship, loyalty and the respect of his whole squad. There's greater longevity in that and everyone wins. He proved it. Keith personified honour and integrity to everyone he came across in football. That proved he did all the important things right and that was all that mattered.

As a young black kid in Nottingham in the 1960s, Keith experienced racism. At that time, careless words and unsavoury actions were commonplace. Worse things happened, too, like the terrible things he'd hear from the terraces. It was there when he grew up and there when he played for some of his many clubs. But as a man and a manager, it was maybe only thereabouts. That was because more people got to know him, and his personality shone through. Lots of people never met him, like fans of other clubs, but they still knew he was a good man. He decided at a very early age that working hard and improving himself was the best way to get on in the world. He would get every qualification he could. Allied with that he had a way about him that won everyone over. So being black was irrelevant, almost unnoticeable, and, to be honest, it's uncomfortable to write about it because to everyone Keith was … just Keith. As many people have said, he wasn't known as a black manager, he was a manager who happened to be black, and the colour of his skin wasn't the thing about him that had any great bearing on anything. His methods and his manner, his humour and his humility were what stood out.

"My dad was my safety net. He would advise me about everything," says Matt Alexander. "He used to tell Paul and I that we wouldn't ever get anything for nothing. We should work hard and we'd get the rewards. And we should watch who we mixed with. He used to say it's OK knowing lots of people but you need to think hard about who you hang about with. My little girl, Remi, has got his photo by her bed. She's only three but she says 'grandad Keith' when you ask her who it is. I've still got his number in my phone. It doesn't seem right to delete it."

Family life was everything to Keith and he often told his players that they should spend all the time they could with theirs. He knew how his family made him keep his football career in perspective and he knew the same thing would work with headstrong young men who needed to be confident but not go off the rails.

"Keith never did a lot of practical things around the house but every Wednesday he cooked the tea," said Helen. "He only did two types of meal – stew or sausages in the slow cooker. The kids always ate every bit. After he died, they let slip that they didn't really like the food that much. They said it tasted a bit funny. I asked them why they ate it then. They said they liked him being there doing it, especially as he was away a lot with work. So they sat and watched him cooking the food, they chatted away to him, then they ate it and never said anything."

When it came to Keith's family it wasn't a case of thereabouts at all. They were there rock-solid, the most important thing in his life. Jack is now fifteen and 6'3". He plays up front for a youth team and, in a few years, he might well be just the sort of player his dad would have raved over. Except his dad wouldn't put pressure on any of his four kids. He'd just guide them and bring them on, helping them to make their own choices but making the right ones based on what they think he would have done. Like he did with his players, his football family. So in a lot of ways, the memories of Keith and the impact he had on a huge number of people aren't thereabouts, they are still firmly there. That's because he made an impression on how to live life and, though he might have gone, that impression will be there for a long time to come.